Cambridge Elements ≡

Elements in Business Strategy
edited by
J.-C. Spender
Kozminski University

A HISTORICAL REVIEW OF SWEDISH STRATEGY RESEARCH AND THE RIGOUR–RELEVANCE GAP

Thomas Kalling
Lund University

Lars Bengtsson
Lund University

CAMBRIDGE
UNIVERSITY PRESS

Shaftesbury Road, Cambridge CB2 8EA, United Kingdom

One Liberty Plaza, 20th Floor, New York, NY 10006, USA

477 Williamstown Road, Port Melbourne, VIC 3207, Australia

314–321, 3rd Floor, Plot 3, Splendor Forum, Jasola District Centre,
New Delhi – 110025, India

103 Penang Road, #05–06/07, Visioncrest Commercial, Singapore 238467

Cambridge University Press is part of Cambridge University Press & Assessment,
a department of the University of Cambridge.

We share the University's mission to contribute to society through the pursuit of
education, learning and research at the highest international levels of excellence.

www.cambridge.org
Information on this title: www.cambridge.org/9781009462358

DOI: 10.1017/9781108648158

First published 2024

A catalogue record for this publication is available from the British Library.

ISBN 978-1-009-46235-8 Hardback
ISBN 978-1-108-46893-0 Paperback
ISSN 2515-0693 (online)
ISSN 2515-0685 (print)

Cambridge University Press & Assessment has no responsibility for the persistence
or accuracy of URLs for external or third-party internet websites referred to in this
publication and does not guarantee that any content on such websites is, or will
remain, accurate or appropriate.

A Historical Review of Swedish Strategy Research and the Rigour–Relevance Gap

Elements in Business Strategy

DOI: 10.1017/9781108648158
First published online: March 2024

Thomas Kalling
Lund University

Lars Bengtsson
Lund University

Author for correspondence: Thomas Kalling, thomas.kalling@fek.lu.se

Abstract: There are many explanations to the so-called rigour–relevance gap in academic research on strategic management. In this Element we review existing literature on the matter and argue that we have to go beyond the typical explanations of knowledge and language differences and look at more fundamental, societal and cultural explanations. The empirical focus of this Element is the history and the possible particularities of strategic management research in Sweden where we show how almost 300 years of relevance-centred research has undergone significant changes over the last 30 years, and that the historical development is based very much on societal pressure, academic culture and shifting perspectives on the role of academic research. We conclude by offering a couple of examples of how Swedish research, close to its traditional approaches, still can contribute to relevance and thus help balance the rigour–relevance divide.

Keywords: strategy, Sweden, rigour, relevance, industry–academy collaboration

ISBNs: 9781009462358 (HB), 9781108468930 (PB), 9781108648158 (OC)
ISSNs: 2515-0693 (online), 2515-0685 (print)

Contents

1 Introduction

The management and administration of business has been taught in various forms and under different labels for centuries. Business strategy is a relatively young subset; its core, as we think of it today, emerged in the 1950s and 1960s as a response to increasing pressure regarding the 'big issues' in the corporate world: long-term decisions, investments, diversification, geographical expansion and so on. In many ways, the strategy discipline has dealt with matters similar to other academic subjects in relation to ontology and epistemology: the view of the world of business, demarcation to adjacent fields, degree of subject integration, uncertainty concerning the object of study, a developing body of fora and outlets, ethical issues and more. In this Element we focus on another topic common to many academic subjects, not least the social sciences: rigour and relevance and the balance between them. We discuss the development of strategy research in Sweden from its inception as an academic subject until today. We single out a single country, albeit a relatively small and marginal one, to understand how, over time, the view on rigour–relevance is impacted by a range of epistemological concerns, the politics of academic governance, the relations between researchers and, not least, the dynamics of the societal and empirical setting. By understanding the longitudinal development of academic research within a specific institutional context, we learn about explanatory factors as well as the consequences of various rigour–relevance strategies.

We connect with the current debate around rigour–relevance in the field of management and strategy and delve into the relatively brief history of strategy research at Swedish universities. We look into the societal context as well as the immediate context of industry and markets; we discuss different theories and methods as well as international relations and empirical instances that are of interest to researchers. We argue that the Swedish example sheds light on a range of reasons why scholars choose (or end up at) a certain position on the rigour–relevance continuum and what might drive the development in either direction.

2 The Rigour–Relevance Debate

Management education and research can be criticised from many different angles. One is that insufficient attention is paid to practical matters or management practice. The rigour–relevance gap (e.g. Starkey & Madan, 2001) has been discussed in various forms among management researchers since the subject of management was introduced at universities. And scholars have debated this not just within the management field, even if management and business administration appear to be particularly exposed to these concerns. Viewpoints have varied depending on the situation. As early as 1918, Thorsten Veblen claimed that business studies 'belongs in the corporation of learning no more than a department of athletics' (Veblen, 1918, pp. 209–10; Engwall et al., 2010). Similar arguments were heard in the 1950s, including Thompson's (1956) claim that much of the literature used in education was 'lore' and that an administrative science must be developed. In 2008, Daft and Lewin argued along the same lines that the fundamental mission of academic journals should be to publish high-quality research 'without regard to relevance of the world of practice' (p. 181). Kieser and Leiner (2009) claimed that management science and management practice are too different from each other, and hence it is impossible to expect both rigour and relevance in research; the two systems can only 'irritate' each other. From the other side of the spectrum, however, particularly in recent times, scholars have argued in favour of the opposite (e.g. Hambrick, 1994; Van de Ven, 2002; Bennis & O'Toole, 2005; Augier & March, 2007; Latham, 2019; Gioia, 2022; Lawler & Benson, 2022): that the lack of relevance in research is detrimental to the education of managers. While the debate has long been simmering, some claim that it has intensified over the last decade (Birkinshaw et al., 2016), with the majority suggesting that relevance has been suffering but that there are ways to bridge the gap. Much of the debate takes place in America, even if Europeans have chipped in to the debate as well. It seems to be a bigger challenge in the American context than in the European – perhaps because Europeans have to a larger extent applied other ontologies and epistemologies, including constructionism, subjectivism and fine-grained empirical studies such as case studies, that have helped offer some level of relevance. There has been European criticism of American approaches in other subject fields, such as organisation, but within strategy Europeans have been keener to buy in to an American approach (although there are exceptions that we will come back to).

Much recent work on rigour–relevance can be said to focus partly on more direct aspects of knowledge differences and the nature of knowledge required in practical or academic contexts. A second angle of criticism of management education and research involves a category of factors that is more macro in character and includes the role of institutional forces for research (and higher education) as well as the relations between academia and industry. Some scholars have attempted to find answers to questions about the rigour–relevance dilemma by looking into historical and genealogical explanations of where we stand with management and strategy. Prominent is Khurana's (2007) history review of business schools.

2.1 Knowledge-Related Differences

Baldridge and colleagues (2004) study the connection between research quality and practical relevance, with relatively disheartening results as the overlap between the two is rather small, thus confirming that there is a significant divide.

They recommend that researchers study challenges to both practice and academia and also apply methods considered valid by practitioners. Most researchers studying the rigour–relevance gap suggest that it is a challenge rooted in questions related to knowledge. Starkey and Madan (2001) argue that one reason behind the lack of relevance is *the nature of the knowledge* produced by academia. Referring to Gibbons and colleagues (1994), they speak about Mode 1 ('conventional' research: homogeneity, disciplinary) and Mode 2 knowledge, where the latter is the result of applied research and characterised by heterogeneity, multidisciplinary approaches and a will to resolve practical problems. According to Starkey and Madan (2001), academic management research has clearly come to focus on Mode 1, and the solutions necessary to balance this in favour of Mode 2 involve radical suggestions such as reorganising universities, their incentive systems and how multi-stakeholder forums form around hot topics, and devising new ways of conceiving 'impact'. They also propose that we review science funding and experiment more with industry–academy collaborations (Starkey and Madan also refer to a prominent Swedish research programme, which we shall come back to).

Likewise, Van de Ven and Johnson (2006) claim that the rigour–relevance gap relates to knowledge. This might be a *knowledge transfer* problem, or a problem in the sense that knowledge of practice and of theory are two *different forms of knowledge*. As argued by Starkey and Madan (2001), a third angle of criticism relates to the process of *knowledge production* (e.g. Mode 1 and Mode 2 knowledge) where the field has clearly opted for Mode 1-type research, while multidisciplinary Mode 2 projects are secondary. Solutions include research questions related to management practice, collaborative communities, multi-methods and rethinking the role of scholarship, orientating it towards clinical approaches with what is termed action research. Similarly, Birkinshaw and colleagues (2016) show that much of what is published by 'bridging media' between the 'worlds of research and practice', such as the *Harvard Business Review*, is inductive or theoretical (rather than statistical/deductive). These papers are often deemed more interesting by practitioners *and* also have high academic impact. Relevance impacts both application and research quality. Gioia (2022) is primarily concerned with the lack of relevance of much management research, and argues that the problem has ontological, epistemological and methodological roots. If we do not understand the differences between the science of the natural and the science of society, we run the risk of failing to understand the object of study, of failing to understand the narratives and perceptions of those managers we study, of failing to communicate how the results of our work can be used. Gioia suggests that it is difficult to be relevant if one does not apply a subjectivist/constructionist approach and an inductive method that truly is rooted in the realities of the actual object of study.

Another area focusing on knowledge transfer is the *evidence-based management* project (e.g. Rousseau, 2006, 2007), which is concerned with the ways in which researchers and others successfully bring tested, evidenced practices into organisations. This may relate partly to the distinction between facts-based decision-making on the one hand and intuition, bias or 'gut feeling', those inexplicable factors that typically form the bases of decisions, on the other. The rise of 'the evidence-based zeitgeist' might appear surprising as this is what managers and consultants (and practice-orientated researchers) have always tried to do, but its increasing popularity signals that something has been missing in our attempts to bring generalised theories into specific contexts. Rousseau (2006) talks about 'Big E Evidence' versus 'little e evidence', where the former refers to generally applicable theory and the latter to locally applicable theory. Rousseau further argues that one part of the problem is the propensity of teachers to alternate by teaching general management skills and using case examples as evidence, when they should instead focus on tested, evidence-based theories that work across cases. Weak research–education links further expand the divide. Solutions for becoming evidence-based include, as suggested by many scholars, promoting active use of evidence-based management and building collaborations among teachers, researchers and practitioners.

2.2 Relations and Institutions

Bartunek (2007) and Bartunek and Rynes (2010) also take a knowledge perspective and show how the 'implications for practice' sections of papers rarely provide practitioners with useful knowledge. One of their solutions is *relational*. They suggest that we look at *integrative scholarship*, that is, research that takes practical concerns seriously and integrates findings within the disciplines into a meaningful whole, where (practice) communities can be researched and related to their everyday concerns. Such scholarship includes textbooks and blogs, consulting, artistic expressions and more. However, as suggested by Bartunek (2007), the practice side probably needs to change too; this might include boundary spanning and relationship building and, by extension, opening up for collaborative research. Bartunek and Rynes (2014) extend the discussion further beyond knowledge and identify a number of tensions connected with the relationships between practitioners and academics. The tensions include *differing logics*, not least when it comes to use of the results of knowledge production, time perspectives, communication forms and both rigour and relevance. They also include *institutional forces*, such as government funding, ranking systems, journal orientation, to which one might add recruitment policy, career management, status and more on the academic side.

Institutional forces on the practitioner side matter too, such as funding, intellectual property (IP) and competition law, and relations to consulting firms.

Another important institutional force in its own right is the subject itself. Agarwal and Hoetker (2007) use industry development theory to describe the evolution of the subject. They scrutinise articles published in the *Academy of Management Journal* (AoMJ) between 1980 and 2005 and observe that the number of citations from outside the management field fell significantly, in favour of references to management research literature itself. Although there were differences according to whether the article in question was of micro or macro nature, in general the once so popular adjacent fields of sociology and economics had become less important, whereas psychology remained strong, particularly in studies at the micro level. They conclude that the subject of management has matured and become a valid discipline in itself. In so doing, it has abandoned much of its multidisciplinary nature and thus lost an important factor behind practical relevance. In the words of Agarwal and Hoetker (2007, p. 1319), the increasing focus over the last decades on discipline and rigour results in 'theoretical and conceptual frameworks that do not inform those who manage firms and lead people'. That subject fields are born and grow in close connection to existing fields is not new; neither is the importance of economics for business administration and management, even if some argue that, originally, the more valid and rigid discipline of economics offered not only content but also academic legitimacy, which management research itself did not have (e.g. Holmqvist, 2018).

The way in which management research has developed is not unique. According to Whitley (1984), subject disciplines typically emerge as disintegrated and dispersed, and with an object of study that is characterised as uncertain. Here one can assume, as a parallel to Agarwal and Hoetker's (2007) findings, that the field is more integrated now compared to the 1950s; consequently, the management field may lack some of its multidisciplinary nature, which in turn might explain why we talk about a greater divide between theory and practice nowadays than ever before. Theoretical parochialism typically drives rigour, not relevance, and logically and as we have already stated, many researchers interested in relevance value the disintegrated nature of management and business administration research precisely because it allows the field to respond more dynamically to emerging matters and concerns (e.g. Engwall, 2020).

2.3 'Scientification'

One of the more prominent studies of the field of management is Rakesh Khurana's (2007) review of the history of American business schools. Many people probably think of the ethical issues addressed by Khurana, but one other matter of significance, at least for the last decades of management research, is declining relevance. Like others, Khurana highlights the importance of the reports known as the 'foundation reports' (by Gordon & Howell, 1959 and Pierson, 1959), which were highly critical of the status of management education at the time, a criticism that naturally spilled over to management research. The authors of the Ford and Carnegie foundation reports (who were all economists) had produced thorough pieces of work (the Ford report was almost 500 pages long) and covered a range of measures including faculty, students, curricula, pedagogics and more. They made observations that the standards were 'embarrassingly low', that it was in violation of the Association to Advance Collegiate Schools of Business (AACSB) standards and that it was mere 'vocational training for trade techniques'. The findings led Gordon and Howell (1959) to question whether business management is a profession – something which had been the mission of institutions such as the AACSB to establish since its inception in the early twentieth century. The resolution suggested was to think of business education as a combination of potentially unrelated disciplines rather than as one coherent subject, where these disciplines typically relied on one or more fundamental subject areas, such as economics, sociology and/or psychology (and also maths, statistics and others). Paired with the strong ambitions to improve the education by applying more rigorous scientific standards, the focus gradually shifted away from the world of the general manager to the world of the specialists (e.g. finance, human resources (HR), marketing). 'Management science' was the new concept, and to the extent that it meant helping the manager, this was done through the daunting task of establishing a broad understanding of a range of different disciplines; the concerns of the manager were translated into set disciplines. Khurana (2007, p. 271) writes: 'In contrast to the old model of business training, this new science would allow managers to make decisions solely on analytical and rational grounds, without recourse to fuzzy notions such as intuition or judgment (the latter being a quality that Harvard Business School explicitly tried to cultivate in its students).'

The foundation reports' recommendations were to increase the proportion of the research faculty, to put a stronger emphasis on quantitative analysis and to develop a clear disciplinary orientation, where hiring from other fields outside of management became the norm; by the mid-1960s, business schools were the major recruiters of graduates in psychology, sociology and economics. Both foundations spent large sums on the business schools that clearly adhered to the new recommendations, including the Graduate School of Industrial Administration (GSIA)/ Carnegie Mellon, which became a model for the future business school. Stanford, Chicago, Wharton, Massachusetts Institute of Technology (MIT) and others followed the recommendations (and were rewarded). Harvard, however, had difficulties adjusting to the new deal, with its general manager-centred programmes. Most importantly, its case-based approach in both education and research was deemed obsolete in the foundation report framework; it was not considered scientific in comparison to the disciplines. Khurana (2007) states that how management problems were resolved in a case was of little interest to the majority of faculty as 'it was assumed that theoretically deduced solutions would be superior anyway'. The business schools' efforts at 'scientification' in the first half of the 1960s were also aided by the formation of scientific societies and their associated journals (compare with the observations by Whitley, 1984 and Agarwal & Hoetker, 2007). Apart from the worldwide standardisation of curricula and disciplines, changes were made to doctoral degrees. The old, practically orientated DBA (doctor of business administration, particularly popular at Harvard) was gradually abandoned in favour of the discipline-orientated PhD (doctor of philosophy). The DBA typically rested on case-based fieldwork with 'real' problems, in clear empirical proximity to the 'real' world. The weight Khurana gives to the two reports when it comes to tilting the continuum towards rigour rather than relevance has been contested. McLaren (2019), for example, argues that Gordon and Howell (1959) and Pierson (1959) cannot bear the sole blame for our current-day propensity to choose rigour over relevance. Many other forces, often of an institutional nature, helped as well: the Cold War (and the idea that the enemy must be met with rigorous, hard science), the maturing of the subject field (compare with Whitley, 1984) and the search for academic legitimacy among emerging business schools are also listed as key factors behind the transformation to the research-based model of education.

According to Khurana (2007), the institutionalisation of the 1960s had some major implications. For one thing, MBA students started to complain about the lack of relevance of the programme, as they were taught theories rather than solutions. Their teachers were now young scientists rather than experienced managers or faculty with business experience, which, for obvious reasons, affected many MBAs. Furthermore, Khurana (2007) argues that the era of institutionalisation also produced managers who were less able to understand the impact of business on society. The increasing orientation towards 'science' and 'discipline' led to the depoliticisation of the profession. Historically, managers in the United States were assumed to, and perhaps did, consider themselves instrumental to American society and its institutions. Students, too, cared less and were more concerned with understanding and using tools and models rather than understanding societal challenges. Teachers did not teach ethics as this was considered outside the scope of disciplines and competence. Khurana (2007) argues that by the end of the 1960s, the foundation reports had 'dramatically transformed American business education' (the only exception being Harvard, which did not fully conform to the Ford model). These forces did not terminate at the end of the 1960s, however. On the contrary, the institutionalisation continued with ever more focus on disciplines rather than general management, which led to a declining interest in the lives of managers. Khurana (2007) lists the recession across many American industries in the early 1970s and the rise of investor capitalism in the mid-1970s as factors or indications that management had lost its status. The shareholder value perspective (Jensen & Meckling, 1976) was an attempt to pit shareholders and managers against each other, exposing corporate management to the market for control. The principal-agent model effectively offered a logic to this arrangement whereby the actions of the chief executive officer (CEO) were expected to be in line with the outcomes defined by the shareholders. This meant rewarding managers to the extent that they delivered on owner ambitions. Management education followed suit and the perception of the general manager became even more like that of a machine, held back not only by subject discipline but also by the stock market. These movements helped push education and research away from the everyday concerns of the general manager. Many people also claim that these were, by extension, major factors behind the divide between rigor and relevance that apparently is still widening.

2.4 The Field of Strategy: Problem and Purpose

Khurana's (2007) historically based argument is compelling, and we have no reason to assume that it does not also apply to the discipline of strategy, even if the debate has been less intensive in strategy than in other disciplines such as HR and organisation studies. Schwenk (1982) discusses strategy research and how we can balance or combine case-based field research and lab experiments, but the more noteworthy observation here at this point in time is that it is perhaps case-based fieldwork that appears to be the norm – not large quantitative studies (and certainly not lab studies). Mintzberg's (1977) perspective assumes case work to be the main form of empirical research, as experiments cannot create conditions similar to real-life decision-making, and suggests that strategy researchers 'have been forced to study real behavior in real organizations, amidst their complexity' (p. 93). Perhaps this indicates that the strategy field had stayed out of at least some parts of the institutionalisation campaigns, at least until the late 1970s. The Harvard case approach still dominated, but things were changing.

A strong statement that there is also a major rigour–relevance divide within strategy surfaced at the Strategic Management Society's (SMS) annual conference in Houston in 2017. Some fifteen or so seasoned scholars (who had all attended the founding 1977 Pittsburgh conference, which came to result in the

SMS) debated the importance of the SMS over the four decades, among other things as an educational resource for practitioners. There appeared to be consensus among panellists that the products of the SMS had very limited value outside the immediate academic circle. Someone stated that 'we have nothing to offer managers nowadays, and they tell us that', and most of the panellists and audience seemed to agree. Most were saddened, but others appeared fine with this state of affairs, reinforcing that the whole point of the SMS was to steer strategy research away from the case-based business policy traditions most notably associated with Harvard Business School. The aim of the *Strategic Management Journal* (SMJ) and the SMS conference, it was stated, had been to make the subject 'more scientific', more 'rigorous', more 'deductive' and more 'quantitative'. Thus, most of the panellists argued that increasingly less relevant ideas had come out of the research conducted within the field. The community had chosen rigour over relevance, and perhaps done it well.

So there seems to be little disagreement about the rigour–relevance divide, even if scholars have different views on whether or not it is in order. The nature of the knowledge, the relations between researchers and those who use the models and, as outlined by Khurana (2007), a range of institutional forces, all play an important part in understanding this. Solutions suggested range from quick-fix efforts such as 'relationship building' to more fundamental takes on institutional change (e.g. funding). Understanding the entire picture around the increasing gap between research and practice requires more than just grasping the practicalities around knowledge, relations and communication. We argue that this is a matter linked to institutional differences across universities as well as differences across businesses and across the societies in which they act. Business administration in general and strategy in particular are two relatively young scientific fields and, furthermore, they were established to help local industry improve and survive in an increasingly competitive environment; consequently, it is not surprising that the first decades or so provided the scientific field with a local touch and local 'recipes'. For better or worse, these differences fade over time as the field matures and becomes truly international, with unified models, theories and methods; they become more integrated, to use Whitley's (1984) terminology. At the same time, as the discipline matures, the impact of the national or the institutional context is eroded. We argue, in this Element, that understanding this dynamic between national, institutional context and the creation of a research community or discourse helps us grasp what can be done to balance rigour and relevance.

We will use the historical development of strategy research in Sweden as an example of said dynamic. The changes described earlier, concerning the way in which rigour has taken over from relevance, have happened in Sweden too.

In that sense, the development in Sweden is not very different from that in the United States; it simply happened later. The Swedish case offers examples of successful relevance approaches in different institutional settings and is therefore interesting as a case. In addition, the Swedish case also offers insights into how a national context can influence not only the research questions but also the methods used and the models generated through empirical research. It is not necessarily the case that the models were intended for Swedish use only; however, they were rooted in a national or local context. Furthermore, the case illustrates how the relations between institutions, such as government, industry and academia, impact all aspects of research. Perhaps the most important contextual factor to bear in mind is that Sweden, like other European countries, has taught and researched areas related to administration and management for centuries. Furthermore, our universities, which came to harbour business education in the twentieth century, are old and include adjacent subject fields; both of these facts have impacted how the subject field is taught and studied. This is not to say that all European institutions are the same; far from it, as we shall see. To summarise, as in other countries, contemporary Swedish strategy research has progressed from empirical proximity in clinic-like arrangements, with a local character and with a high degree of relevance, much in sync with society *and* history, to join an integrated global body of strategy researchers where scientific rigour and generally applicable theory are the norm. In the process of these changes, we think we can find an answer, or at least an illustration, to what happens as we lose relevance in favour of rigour. However, the Swedish strategy tradition also holds several examples, from the early days and more recently, of what can be done to balance rigour and relevance. So we argue that the management of the research–practice divide is better understood if placed in a comparative context, but also in a broader historical setting. As stated in Section 1, the purpose is to shed light on why we take certain positions on the rigour–relevance continuum and how these choices can be managed. As empirical material, we discuss the history of strategy research in Sweden.

3 Strategy Research in Sweden

In the following section, we discuss the Swedish case of strategy research. We start by discussing the contextual background to it, namely the introduction of the mother subject of business administration into university curricula; we also discuss the societal characteristics and academic norms and values that came to shape strategy research, at least in the early phases. We then turn to discussion of the different contributions made by Swedish scholars. We have, however, divided this discussion into an early and a late era because we argue that there is a dividing line, albeit a blurry one at times, between the early and subsequent works. Many characteristics prevail, but others change, such as the purpose of research projects, the focus of the models spawned (and used), the balance between helping managers and producing research respected by fellow academics. We have therefore structured the empirical account of Swedish research to include not only the early and the later eras but also the 'transition period' where we discuss some of the answers to why rigour came to overtake relevance.

3.1 Contextual Background

In this review, we start by discussing the contextual background against which business administration came to be a subject and an element of university curricula and then we look at how societal characteristics, along with subject-related preference for theory, method and purpose, came to shape strategy research in Sweden.

3.1.1 The History of Administration in Sweden

As in many other European countries, what might be considered administration has been taught at universities for centuries. In Sweden, one of the earliest scholars within the field (alongside Schefferus at Uppsala) was Samuel von Pufendorf, a German historian and philosopher of law who had accepted a position as chair in natural jurisprudence at the newly inaugurated university in Lund in 1668. He later moved to become historiographer at the court in Stockholm. Pufendorf was not primarily an economist, but he made contributions to the field of natural rights and also value, state and taxation. Although not as practically orientated as his cameralist successors, he made significant contributions to the field of economics and administration; he believed in the market, but like many of his countrymen was a proponent of state control and regulation of commercial activities, in order to avoid exploitation and depletion of natural resources (Magnusson, 1992). His main work is *De Jure Naturae et Gentium* (Pufendorf, [1688]/1934) in which he attempts to combine Grotius' and Hobbes' ideas on international and natural law. Adam Smith referred repeatedly to Pufendorf's works on natural rights in his Lectures in Jurisprudence (delivered in Glasgow in 1762–3) and Rousseau later recommended Pufendorf's work for inclusion in law curricula.

Pufendorf left Sweden in 1688 to return to Berlin, to the court of King Friedrich and later King Friedrich Wilhelm, in the House of Prussia. Irrespective of whether he had any influence on the kings, Pufendorf came to Berlin at a time when the view of commerce, mercantilism and industry was about to change. The German cameralist movement was born out of Friedrich Wilhelm's increasing desire to rationalise the Prince's treasury (*kammer*) in the early eighteenth century. Friedrich Wilhelm was not the only principal in Europe faced with these challenges, but was probably the most successful. He was disappointed with the competence levels of the civil servants, who were predominantly trained in the law, and their incapacity for economic analysis and action. Principals, politicians and mercantilists wanted to see economic education on the university curricula because of the prospect of generating wealth (Wakefield, 2005). Chairs were established at the Prussian universities of Halle and Frankfurt an der Oder in the 1720s, and the movement later reached Sweden. Uppsala established the first chair in 1741, which was occupied by Anders Berch; Åbo (which was then Swedish) established a chair in 1747; and Lund installed its first professor, Burmester, in 1750 (Magnusson, 1992). These appointments were evidence of a desire among the powers that be to rationalise trade, public and private organisation, and the management of raw materials such as agriculture, mining, forestry, hydropower and more. Heads of state and governments saw a desperate need for trained administrators because of the potential economic improvements. To many, cameralist academic activity in the eighteenth century appeared to be a mixture of practical engineering (recommendations and checklists for how to manage farms, iron mines and so on) and economics in the household management sense. In Sweden (this was the Age of Liberty and Enlightenment) academic naturalists such as Celsius, Linnaeus and Polhem and practitioners such as Macklean (who pioneered the *enskiftet*, farmland rationalisation through the integration of scattered acres) were representatives of this movement and achieved considerable success in their respective fields. Similar movements also happened elsewhere in Scandinavia (Monsen, 2002).

Cameralism in Germany and Scandinavia has been dubbed 'reform mercantilism' (Magnusson, 1987) as, in comparison to the less restricted British and Dutch mercantilism, it included the idea that government control of trade and industry could actually benefit enterprise and the economy and have positive long-term effects. Berch (1749) was a staunch advocate for government control of commerce and the exploitation of natural resources, and Magnusson (1987) summarises Berch's view as one in which 'the unrestricted forces of a free market economy represent a primitive stage of development, while civilization corresponds to rational government and the use of statecraft to develop and modernize' (p. 428). Cameralism was a strong force at the universities in Sweden up until the mid-nineteenth century. And, as later, there was tension between cameralist academics and practitioners (books and bureaus in Wakefield's (2005) terminology) and between cameralist academics and other academics. Nonetheless, it helped Sweden develop as a nation of trade and industry, and it undoubtedly laid the foundations not only in society but also at the universities to prepare for and enjoy the benefits of industrialisation. The subject gradually faded out in the mid-nineteenth century but was partly reborn towards the end of the century when Lund and Uppsala began to recruit economists, including David Davidson in Uppsala and Knut Wicksell in Lund. These economists, however, were less interested in (the mundane matters associated with) administration and management.

Yet the subject area of business administration as we know it today gradually took off in the early 1900s, partly through the inauguration of the Stockholm School of Economics (SSE) in 1909 and its counterpart in Gothenburg in 1923. Both were funded privately by representatives of banks (SSE) and trade (Gothenburg) and, like an echo from the past, came about primarily to cater for the increasing need for qualified administrators in industry and trade. Much like the experience in other European countries, the established universities and faculties resisted, strongly, the suggestion that they should include business studies. In Sweden, Veblen's statement (see Section 2) was repeated as academics suggested that it was inappropriate for universities to offer 'courses of use for practical life' (Engwall, 1986, p. 123; see also Engwall et al., 2010).

The primary orientation was accounting and bookkeeping, but this would subsequently be expanded. Concurrently, administration was also taught on a modest scale at applied institutions such as colleges of forestry and agriculture, as well as at the Royal Institute of Technology and the Chalmers Institute of Technology (Engwall, 1986). The first chair at the SSE was appointed in 1915, after which little happened. At the end of the 1940s, there were still only six chairs in business administration in Sweden. The first *oeconomiae doctor* in business administration was Nils Västhagen, who defended his thesis in accounting at Gothenburg in 1950 and then took up a professorship at the SSE in 1951 before moving to Lund to take up the first chair there, in 1958.

So the subject of business administration was clearly emerging as we approached the 1950s, at which point the established universities were unable to refrain from absorbing it any longer. Whereas business had been taught in law departments on a small scale, government efforts throughout the first part of the twentieth century to introduce it as a subject had failed owing to a shortage of teaching capacity and resistance from existing faculty. However, in 1953 a government committee concluded that business administration could be studied at university, both from a social science perspective and from an applied perspective, and recommended that chairs be created at Lund and Uppsala. Both departments of business administration were founded in 1958, and after a period of various faculty affiliations the departments were integrated into their respective faculties of social science. Stockholm

University and Umeå University created their departments of business administration in 1964 and 1965, respectively.[1]

Historically, at least up until World War II, Sweden was no stranger to mimicking German institutions, but this was not the case when it came to the early days of business administration.[2] Unlike the Germans, who turned their *Handelshochschulen* [business schools] into universities early in the twentieth century, the Swedes left doing this until the latter half of the century. Furthermore, research and science were not given the same prominence at Swedish universities as they received in Humboldtian Germany as early as the nineteenth century (Locke, 1985). For the first half of the 1900s, Sweden was more like France, with independent, private business schools that were governed by private and local interests, typically associations of commerce, with the practical bias that follows. It was not until later, with the maturing of the SSE and Gothenburg and the introduction of business administration at the regular state-controlled universities, that Sweden took on a more German approach to academic research, but it is difficult to see a causal relation; by the time business administration peaked in Sweden, in the 1950s and 1960s, America was clearly the ideal and the source of inspiration; Germany certainly was not. One area where Sweden came to resemble (at least pre-war) Germany later was in defining the scope of the subject; Swedish institutions, like their German but unlike their American counterparts, which specialised more gradually, had a broader view of the subject of business administration, albeit with a base orientation towards accounting.

The interest in business administration was driven by the demands not only of industry and trade but also of the public sector. There was a need for competent administrators who had not only mastered bookkeeping but could also take decisions on distribution, marketing and finance. Firms, including Swedish firms, grew and became complex creatures through internationalisation and divisionalisation. The Marshall Plan fuelled the economy and demand. The global (and Western) society was occupied with post–World War II modernisation in terms of consumption, infrastructure development, urbanisation and more. Government spending increased steadily and Keynesian economics was the dominant norm, not least in Sweden where the Social Democrats ruled without interruption from 1932 to 1976. The Social Democrats had a firm belief in the role of industry and capitalism and introduced what came to be known as 'the middle way' (Childs, 1936), where market and planned economy coexist.

---

[1] *This historical review owes much to Lars Engwall's (1986) thorough account of the history of business administration in Sweden.*

[2] *Sweden did mimic the German cameralist movement in the eighteenth century, as discussed earlier in this section.*

The purpose behind the creation of the new business education was in part to improve management of Swedish organisations, and models and ideas tended to come out of reflections of contemporary challenges to Swedish industry and society. This, in turn, was probably partly related to the fact that representatives from industry had a strong interest in the education programmes and sat on advisory boards and the like, or served as assistant professors or even full-time teachers. Generally, there was a significant overlap of industry and academy at the young Swedish institutions.

3.1.2 Societal and Intra-subject Influences

The Swedish academic strategy tradition reflects – at least, it did initially – the nature and the condition of Swedish society. As Sweden is a nation that is heavily reliant on international trade and openness and has an institutional ideology that rests on the assumptions that market forces are good if paired with ideas of redistribution, regulation and taxation, that firms are each but one institution among many, and that consensus and collaboration are the lifeblood of society and essential features of decision-making, it is not surprising that its models for corporate strategy reflected this. During the first decades of strategy research, there was also an engineering ethos suggesting that strategy research and education were there to help improve things and that this was controllable and achievable through wise analysis, planning and leadership. As indicated earlier, this optimism was one central reason why business administration was being introduced and taught at universities. Here, we identify a set of six societal and academic themes that clearly made their mark on strategy research in Sweden during the formative years.

1 Internationalisation

Firstly, Sweden is a small, highly *export-dependent* country with a long history of overseas trade, including with both the Vikings and later the East Indian trading companies (Sweden was never a successful coloniser). Ericsson and other Swedish firms were established with offices outside Europe during the nineteenth century. Swedish raw material suppliers (e.g. iron, forestry products), manufacturers of steel, automobiles, pharmaceuticals, machinery and equipment, paper, electronics and others have strived throughout the twentieth century, and particularly from the post–World War II era, to find new ways of getting their products out. For the greater part of the twentieth century, Sweden had a positive trade balance with its European neighbours, but after the war, exports to the rest of the world, too, increased. And the farther away you export, the more likely you are to encounter challenges associated with cultural, institutional and demographic differences. So, in light of those processes, it is not surprising that it was in Sweden that researchers developed the Uppsala internationalisation model (Johanson & Vahlne, 1977), one of the most influential theoretical frameworks of the firm's internationalisation process in the field of international business for more than forty years (Vahlne & Johanson, 2017; Vahlne, 2020).

2 Systemic Models

Secondly, one prominent feature of Swedish society and strategy research at the time was a holistic, *systemic* approach, which includes aspects of both consensus and collaboration, and in consequence augmented macro views on society and business. What became known as the Swedish model, the middle way, requires *consensus* and a willingness to unite behind large-scale agreements, in some cases arch-agreements (that determine how to settle minor agreements). This meant that macro relations became dependent upon a genuine will to collaborate. Many claim that the origins of the middle way lie in the *Saltsjöbadsavtalet* [Saltsjöbaden Agreement] of 1938 between the labour unions and the employers' confederation, which regulated the handling of labour market conflicts, including strike rights and the like. The spirit of the Saltsjöbaden Agreement has lived on in Swedish society. The Saltsjöbaden Agreement, in turn, cannot be fully understood without understanding the Swedish *Folkhemmet* [people's home] model, introduced in the late 1920s by the Social Democrats just before taking office. The *Folkhemmet* model was a perspective on the state and society, partly influenced by the introduction of social insurance in Prussia in the mid-1800s by Otto von Bismarck, where the home and the family became the general metaphor for societal development. The idea was not only to reduce or eliminate class differences, and to modernise by moving away from feudal Sweden, but also to develop a society where the free market and government intervention coexisted, and where a strong redistribution system would guarantee economic equality.

The privileged institutions, including influential capitalists, accepted and bought into these changes. In return they gained other privileges, including influence in economic policy (for the capitalists) combined with direct business with government institutions and agencies. Privately owned companies, such as Ericsson, Saab, Asea/ABB and the construction industry, among others, would not be what they are today had agencies such as the Ministry of Defence, the national telecom operator (Televerket), the national utility provider (Vattenfall), Swedish Rail and others not bought their products and helped specify advanced solutions. In this national context, and in the light of the densely connected society that came with Keynesian economic policy, it is perhaps not surprising that systemic approaches such as the stakeholder model were launched in Sweden (Rhenman & Stymne, 1965).

With consensus came a focus on collaboration and cooperation. Swedish firms and management in general are perhaps less competitive in their approach compared to American colleagues; management is often considered a matter not primarily of bargaining or of fiercely competing with rivals but rather of developing the organisation and staff and nurturing external and internal relations. Here, Sweden is closer to what Chandler (1990) refers to as the German 'cooperative managerial capitalism'. The interest in 'consonance' (e.g. Normann, 1969) and later in inter-organisational relations (e.g. Larsson et al., 1998) and 'coopetition' (e.g. Bengtsson & Kock, 2000, 2014) is reflective of this. As a consequence of the collaborative character, it is not surprising that many Swedish models of strategy are macro, with systemic features and complex interrelations between factors, and an *augmented view* of the firm. The stakeholder model is a case in point, as is the business idea concept (Normann, 1971). There are strong connections, too, between the models emerging in Sweden and the contingency perspective (e.g. Lawrence & Lorsch, 1967), namely, that stakeholders and the business idea must be understood as a mutually interdependent complex of subsystems involving 'the organisation' and 'the environment'. Few Swedish strategy researchers have had a strong inclination to test connections between individual variables; they tend instead to construct (potentially complex – and coarse) frameworks for analytical purposes.

3 Engineering Ethos and Controllability

Thirdly, another prominent feature then, which is perhaps more important to note as it is less prominent today, was the 'engineering ethos', the belief that things can improve, and this belief was strengthened by an increasing sensation of controllability. Figure 1 shows the output volumes of Volvo Cars from its inception in 1927 until the end of the century. The wealth of Volvo Cars is a good symbol and representative of the Swedish economy in general, not least as Volvo Cars sourced a great deal of its input from other Swedish suppliers, both small industries in the countryside and steelworks in the north. As is evident, the post–World War II years, fuelled by the Marshall Plan and other financial injections into the system, gave Volvo Cars and the entire economy a fascinating development curve that remained unbroken for approximately a quarter of a century, until the oil crisis in 1973. The remarkable thing about this section of the growth curve is not only the northbound tendency but also the stability and the *controllability*. We are talking 5 per cent to 10 per cent

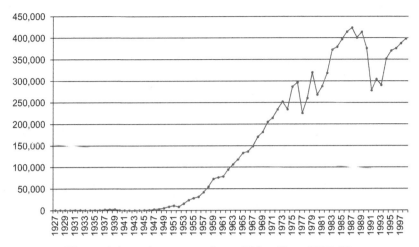

Figure 1 Annual turnover of cars, Volvo Cars, 1927–99.

manageable growth per year, no more, no less, which in itself emphasises the plausibility of long-term strategic planning. It is not surprising that throughout the 1950s and 1960s decision-makers in both private and public sectors were optimistic about the future and, over time, grew used to planning contexts where there were few clouds in the sky. The early strategy-related works of Swedish contemporaries are examples of this (Rhenman, 1961, 1962; Carlson, 1964; Rhenman & Stymne, 1965). The oil crisis was followed by recessions, cyclicality and, in the 1980s, deregulation; these historical events created a more varied and heterogeneous world of business, nudging research towards becoming more specialised.

The close interaction between industry and academy, particularly in the early days of the 1960s and 1970s, came from a broad wish in society to be better and more competitive. The quality of the Swedish administrative corps was allegedly not overly impressive in the 1950s, and increasing international competition led to pressure to start educating and preparing people for leadership and administration. Strategy and management teachers were tasked with helping students understand the milieu and the nature of the work of the executive (Carlson, 1964, is a very good example) and in order to succeed they needed to be acquainted with said environments. When Richard Normann (1971) was published in the ASQ at the age of twenty-seven, this was greeted with a yawn by his contemporaries, who were more interested in solving practical problems than in writing about them. Throughout the 1960s, the business admin scholar was more of a teacher or consultant than a researcher.

4 Idiographic Research Approach

One characteristic that has prevailed in Swedish strategy research, with only a few exceptions, is the *idiographic research* approach that emphasises rich descriptions, that is to say multi-aspect, in-depth and process case studies and conceptual work with theory development ambitions. One rarely finds a nomothetic research approach, by which we mean research emphasising quantitative analysis of a few aspects across large samples to test hypotheses and make statistical generalisations. This might be owing to the inability or the ignorance of Swedish researchers. They simply seem keener on conceptual development or case work – the immediate roots to this approach are probably a mix of the clinical and relevance-seeking efforts of the pioneers in Sweden and the fact that much that was written in the early days was intended not to be published in scientific journals but to serve as teaching material or feedback reports to clients. Furthermore, it might be related to the fact that many of the influential pieces on strategy that were published internationally in the early days were not about statistics; rather, they were conceptual or case-based (compare with Selznick, 1957; Penrose, 1959; Chandler, 1962; and Andrews et al., 1965). No Swedish strategy researcher, to our knowledge, has referred to themselves as standing on either side in the German–Austrian *Methodenstreit* [method dispute] (Grimmer-Solem, 2003), but we would argue that the Swedish business administration and strategy traditions typically side with Gustav von Schmoller in the German camp, where induction and historicism take centre stage alongside holistic societal considerations. Contingent and (spatially and temporally) contextualised case studies, with explicit ambitions to learn from them while also (typically) helping study objects develop, were, at least in the early days, the dominant norm for strategy research in Sweden. There are exceptions with more typical statistical approaches, such as Pehrsson (2006), but, in general, influential statistical studies are notably scarce in Swedish strategy research. Rikard Larsson's case survey approach (e.g. Larsson, 1993; Larsson & Finkelstein, 1999) is principally a statistical method, but based on the reinterpretation of case data collected, analysed and published by others.

A respectable body of literature by Swedes centres on methodological choices; Sune Carlson (1964) uses almost half the space in his book to explain, in detail, his data collection method. Normann (1976), Lind and Rhenman (1989) and Stymne (1995) are but three examples of the many pieces that have defended the clinical research method applied by, among others, Scandinavian Institute for Administrative Research (SIAR) researchers. Later, Larsson (1993), among others, discussed the differences between idiographic (Europe) and nomothetic (North America) research, the merits of the two approaches and also how they could be combined. We will return to this in Section 3.3.6.

5 Process Perspectives

A second characteristic of strategy research in Sweden is the strong orientation towards processes; Swedes have clearly been more interested in processes, both managerial and organisational. With a couple of noteworthy exceptions, the approach is typically a longitudinal, process-based Mintzbergian view of strategy, rather than, say, a cross-sectional, content or position-based Porterian view (Bengtsson et al., 1997). Rhenman's early work was influenced by other more behaviouristic approaches, such as those by Simon, by March and by Selznick. In the 1970s and onwards, Mintzberg (e.g. 1978, 1987) was an important source of inspiration, as were Quinn (1978) and the Bower–Burgelman framework (e.g. Bower, 1970; Burgelman, 1983, 1988). To some, although not necessarily the figureheads themselves (e.g. Whittington, 2007), the strategy-as-practice perspective (e.g. Whittington, 2006; Johnson et al., 2007) was seen as an extension of the strategy process view and became relatively popular (with Leif Melin as the obvious front figure in Sweden), although perhaps more so among regular organisation scholars than strategists.

So, most strategy research from Sweden is process-orientated, from the early days of the 1960s up until today. Models have a time component and with that a dynamic, realist and problem-orientated character. In general, the orientation is definitely towards the longitudinal processes of decision-making and implementation, and the cognitive, cultural and political issues that follow. Assumptions frequently include bounded rationality, opportunism, distrust, stupidity, political divides, barriers of language, culture, knowledge, motivation and all the other features that underline the fact that strategic development is not a linear, rational process. Early Swedish strategy researchers strongly believed at the time that understanding decision-making could not solely be a matter of economic deliberation; rather, it had to be a more sociological or psychological affair that is best studied over time, longitudinally. So, for example, the relationship between strategy and economics was arduous during the 1960s and 1970s. Staunch positivist economists did not consider strategy or management to be a science, as it would not lend itself well to cross-sectional statistical enquiry. Strategists, on the other hand, would suggest, with a Freudian wink, that economists were suffering from 'physics envy'. In Lund, for example, business students defending their PhD dissertations could rest assured that professors from the economics department would show up at the public disputation and try aggressively (and sometimes successfully) to rip the rookies to pieces. In many ways this conflict, again, was a *Methodenstreit* in miniature format.

6 Purpose: Improvement

A third characteristic, related not so much to theory or to method but rather to purpose, was a desire to provide relevant and useful models that had been used and proven useful in actual client cases. The ambition to be relevant to practitioners used to be stronger. This is evident in the works of the SIAR associates – in the sense that they developed analytical models, such as the stakeholder model, the business idea model and the services framework, that were aimed directly at decision-makers (political or corporate) – as well as most of the others during the early era. 'Practical implications' was not just the heading of an empty paragraph at the end of texts, such as it might be today; it was the actual purpose of projects (compare with Bartunek & Rynes, 2010). This is evident partly but not primarily in publications, and definitely in the many client reports that, for example, SIAR would generate. There are probably many reasons why relevance was more important, relatively, in the early days. First, the calibre of Swedish management was apparently not up to standard. This was part of the reason why the Swedish government invested so heavily in management education at the time. Second was probably the fact that many young students who would otherwise have gone into engineering chose business administration. One could perhaps assume that the general zeitgeist of the era, with soaring post–World War II growth, created a social space for youngsters to join the modern project. Third, post–World War II firms were growing in scale, scope and geographic presence. Marketing, sales, distribution – and management – were added to accounting. As indicated in the section 'Engineering Ethos and Controllability', the quarter of a century from the 1940s up until the oil crisis provided fertile ground for planning as it was an era of stable growth. In such a context, it was not surprising that a subject such as strategy was so attractive to any normatively inclined young student.

Fourth, the creation of research groups with a strong focus on *administration* as opposed to *production* was also testament to a new perspective and a new ambition, to understand and improve the life of the decision-maker. These groups and institutes were also a hideaway from the academic corridors where, as we discussed earlier, some of the antipathy against business administration existed. According to Stymne (1995), it was important for SIAR to get away from the SSE in order to pursue its own line of 'clinical research', to help solve client problems and afterwards consider and elaborate on the learnings. Rhenman thought that existing management research was unfit for the real problems and challenges that business leaders were facing. In addition, he was unimpressed by the gradual differentiation of the field of business administration into disciplines, as he felt that researchers missed the holistic issues that the manager had to deal with

(Stymne, 1995). From its start in the 1950s and up until the mid- to late 1980s, we would argue, the main aim of academic research was still to help firms improve and managers understand their world and make the right decisions. A good strategy scholar was one who could also 'operate on the patient'.

Conclusions

As indicated already, we suggest that six societal and academic characteristics influence Swedish strategy research. Some of these prevail throughout the period since the 1950s, while others are stronger at times. The main point here is that the idea of controllability and the associated engineering ethos and quest for relevance gradually fade as we transit from the early to the late era. So, to some extent, does the systemic nature of models; we gradually increase the focus on 'minor' instances and variables (resources, capabilities, positions, etc.) at the expense of the 'big picture' matters that might concern general management. The idiographic research approach is a component of almost all research in both eras. So if we look at the *early era*, it is characterised by systemics, process and an international outlook. What is noteworthy about the early era is that while different universities share the idiographic approach and the quest for relevance, they specialise in one of systemics, process and internationalisation, even when they typically had a little of all three. Lund and the SIAR school came to focus on systemics, whereas Gothenburg and Linköping focused on process, and Uppsala and the SSE on internationalisation questions. Later, these geographical specialisations were less clear.

3.2 The Early Era

In the following we describe what we refer to as the early era, in which we include early pieces by some of the early scholars in Sweden. In fact, it was so early that the concept of strategy was not really used. It is difficult to state whether a paper belongs to strategy, particularly in the early days before the concept was used. Many people might claim that we have forgotten important work; others might think that we have wrongly positioned their work as strategy. We have included works that are often referred to by other strategy researchers and works that clearly deal with explanations for performance, competition and decision-making, but organisation and marketing scholars, among others, might think that we are occasionally walking on thin ice with our definitions. Unsurprisingly, perhaps, there are fewer institutions involved in the early era, simply because not all the departments in Sweden had been established and made breakthroughs until later. In this early period, we touch base with Lund, Uppsala, Stockholm, Gothenburg and Linköping.

3.2.1 SIAR: A Systemics Approach

Formed by Eric Rhenman and others in 1966 in Stockholm, SIAR was a research institute funded by external grants outside the university system and whose mission was to do research commissioned by industry and other partners. Many of the researchers at that time were employed by universities, frequently the SSE, and had already had experience of doing research in industry-academia constellations. As Rhenman was made a preceptor (a level just below full professor) in Lund that same year,[3] he moved there and brought SIAR with him; for most people in the field, SIAR is associated with Lund, even though it went on to become not only a very successful research institute but also a successful consulting firm, with its academic approach a unique feature among the competition. Although the research component eventually vanished, SIAR's impact on Swedish and international management thinking was significant, at least up until the mid-1970s.

Rhenman had double degrees (in chemistry from the Royal Institute of Technology and in business administration from the SSE) and found his first job at Esso (the Swedish branch of Standard Oil) in 1955. He soon moved to AB Atomenergi, a government-controlled company doing research on nuclear power and nuclear arms. For many young hotshots, nuclear physics was the industry to be in at the time, following Eisenhower's Atoms for Peace initiative and the Manhattan project in the United States. Rhenman's job was to assist the CEOand to make suggestions related to the organisation and control of operations. Rhenman stayed with AB Atomenergi until 1964 but took numerous breaks to further his studies, gaining, among other things, a licentiate degree from the SSE. He taught there and also visited Carnegie Tech in Pittsburgh and Cambridge University in the UK. In 1964, he had the opportunity to start his own research group, the GAU (Gruppen för Administrativt Utvecklingsarbete [Group for Administrative Development Work]), at the SSE. Its task was to do commissioned research for client institutions, something Rhenman and others had already been doing for some time, and which had been the foundation for the texts Rhenman had written in the late 1950s and early 1960s.

Administration

The first of the research areas Rhenman was involved in was administration, which in many ways was a way to take a stand against production, the dominant area at that time. The steel, forest, energy and manufacturing industries were up and running and Swedish firms were expanding internationally, as well as in

---

[3] *This section on Eric Rhenman relies heavily on his biography by Carlsson (2013) and interviews with his associates, conducted by the authors.*

size. Many of them were suffering from growing pains and teething problems, and so the need for management ideas and analytical tools was significant.

It is in this context that Rhenman developed his initial ideas and perspectives on business. His licentiate thesis (Rhenman, 1961) included four articles with a mixed approach to management (including a paper on management games as well as an exhaustive review of the field of organisation theory, including all the classics). The paper that stands out and marks Rhenman's position as a scholar of administration is that on the organisation as a control system, an edited version of which was later published as *Det administrerande systemet. En organisationsmodell* [The organisation as a control system] (Rhenman, 1962). His immediate influence is primarily Simon (1947) and March and Simon (1958). Rhenman suggests that we must separate productive processes from administrative ones. It is noteworthy that this early piece by Rhenman has strong proximity with the cognitive and artificial intelligence features of Simon's framework, as well as operations analysis and general systems theory – things he criticises elsewhere.[4] The sociological and ideological flavour of, for example, Selznick is not yet in place, and norms, values, goals and objectives do not yet take centre stage. Rhenman was probably also considered radical by his peers because his thesis did not include the typical statistical tests of hypotheses but was geared towards practical problems.

The Stakeholder Model

In the early 1960s, the Swedish Confederation of Employers (SAF [Svenska Arbetsgivareföreningen]) invited Rhenman to help develop teaching material for courses offered to their members on the topic of rationalisation. This resulted in the book *Rationaliseringsarbete. Organisering och Planering [Rationalisation Work – Organisation and Planning]* (Ahlmann & Rhenman, 1964). More importantly, though, he gained connections at the confederation that would later lead to the project that resulted in a book and a model that are perhaps his most famous contribution to the field of management and strategy. Rhenman was asked to join a committee to outline the premises under which employers should approach the delicate matter of corporate democracy and the influence of blue-collar and white-collar unions in corporate decision-making processes. The democratisation of the

---

[4] *He wrote his licentiate papers in the late 1950s while at Carnegie, and took PhD courses from both Simon and March. At the time, Rhenman was moving away from positivist, engineering approaches that carried even the faintest hints of operations analysis, towards the 'softer' approaches and methods of social sciences and sociology, such as hermeneutics and phenomenology. Rhenman did not receive the response from Simon that he expected, so Simon recommended that Rhenman contact Selznick – described as one of Simon's critics but the one that Simon himself respected the most. Rhenman met with Selznick; while Selznick was uninterested, he gave Rhenman a long rendition of his ideas on organisation, which had a strong impact.*

workplace had been a hot topic in Sweden since the 1920s. The Saltsjöbaden Agreement of 1938 had been considered a success, but by now both parties felt an increasing urge to review the principles of conflict resolution. Rhenman's job within the committee was to write a thesis outlining the corporate perspective on workplace democracy. As stated in the foreword of the book that was subsequently published (Rhenman, 1964, p. ix): 'The questions that the debate about a democratisation of the workplace highlights have been described and analysed from many perspectives, including politics, sociology, social psychology, policy and labour law. The purpose of this book is to show that these questions can also be described and understood from the perspective of corporate organisation.'

To Rhenman, the solution was a balance of interests between the corporation's stakeholders.[5] Here, stakeholders include the corporate management, owners, employees, customers and suppliers (as in a typical input-process-output model), as well as government (local, regional, national and federal) and legislators (there is no mention of media, which is perhaps testament to the growing importance this interest has enjoyed over the last fifty years). Stakeholders are to some extent voluntary members, and it is likely that their ambitions and objectives vary. The main task for the corporate management is to make sure they meet as many of the objectives of the stakeholders as possible. This requires conflict resolution, as all objectives cannot be met simultaneously. It illustrates clearly the many difficulties inherent in corporate decision-making. In Rhenman and Stymne (1965), the model is referred to as the Contribution–Reward model, which covers the reasons why stakeholders remain in or around an organisation, or leave.

The stakeholder model is interesting for many reasons. It is highly emblematic of the times, when the Swedish economy was booming and the labour market parties were concerned about the distribution of wealth. In that sense, it positions itself at the very heart of a societal Swedish debate during the twentieth century. However, although the message was that the labour market parties and the corporate stakeholders should be, and were, able to regulate their relations through mutual interdependency, without interference by law, ten years later Sweden passed a number of bills that regulated and clarified the influence of the unions and the safety of employees, including the Employment Act (1974) and later the Co-Determination Act (1976), which clearly improved the possibilities for employees to realise their interests.

Scientifically, the stakeholder model can be used to determine performance and survival, but it has perhaps not been very prominent in strategy theory, even

---

[5] *The Swedish word for 'stakeholder' is* intressent – *someone with an interest – and so in Swedish the model is known as* Intressentmodellen.

if it clearly attempts to understand organisational survival. There are, however, exceptions, including Ed Freeman's (1984, 2010) approach to strategic management, which continue to cite Rhenman's pioneering work of the 1960s. Rhenman's view has become popular on and off over the years, most notably perhaps in the more recent discussions of corporate responsibility. In a model where fulfilment of the objectives of the principal and compliance with the law are the only responsibilities of firms (e.g. Friedman, 1970), the impact of corporate actions on the broader instances of societies are neglected, but the stakeholder model can remedy such bias. As far as Rhenman himself was concerned, the project and the book received a lot of attention in the Swedish media, and he gained a reputation that helped form the GAU and SIAR. This continued throughout the late 1960s and culminated perhaps in his 1969 book *Företaget och dess omvärld. Organisationsteori för långsiktsplanering [The Corporation and Its Environment: Organisation Theory for Long-Term Planning]*, in which Rhenman clearly takes a broader perspective on 'management' and suggests that 'our society has the corporations and corporate leaders it deserves' (Rhenman, 1969a, pp. 11–12).

A Strategy Turn

Rhenman was inspired by contingency theory and started empirical work on two seemingly unrelated questions: organisation planning, a purely conceptual approach, and the management and administration of hospitals, which was empirically orientated. The studies resulted in two books published in 1968 (*Organisationsplanering [Organisation Planning]*) and 1969 (*Centrallasarettet [The Central Hospital]*) (Rhenman, 1968, 1969b). The latter came to form the backbone of SIAR's subsequent work on hospital organisation and management. It was also a first marker of SIAR's orientation towards seeing sectors and industries as unique and difficult to compare. With its contingency perspective, and a methodological perspective that suggests that firms and industries are unique, it was clear to the group that a case-based, almost phenomenological approach to organisation was necessary. *Organisationsplanering*, on the other hand, was perhaps one of the first (almost) purely practical pieces on how to design organisations, including structure, control, work, responsibility and so on. It was based on simulations of three real-life cases and reported on the ways in which three 'planners' designed their organisations. One of the general insights was the suggestion that organisations are inherently unique; their norms and values have been developed over time, and the external environment differs across industries, in an important way. In that sense, these two studies from the mid-1960s have a lot more in common than one might assume.

Following the success of the corporate democracy project, Rhenman also assumed his tenured position in the Department of Business Administration at Lund University in 1966, which was converted into a professorship in 1967. By this time, he had fallen out with the SSE, largely owing to differences in their respective views on more or less all aspects of research. Following this, GAU was transformed into the independent foundation SIAR, which gave Rhenman and his co-founders an independent platform from which to pursue their research.

The Business Idea: The Firm and Its Environment

With *Företaget och dess omvärld. Organisationsteori för långsiktsplanering [The Corporation and Its Environment: Organisation Theory for Long-Term Planning]*, Rhenman (1969a) launched the concept of 'systems for domination', which was later developed into the 'business idea' concept. This is also one of the first times that Rhenman uses the concept of 'strategy'. He is able to apply his full repertoire of concepts, but he also allows his underlying assumption about harmony between systems and subsystems to surface. This is perhaps also the most blatant Selznickian (particularly the 1957 piece [Selznick, 1957]) of Rhenman's publications. The idea that the firm is infused with value and that successful firms become institutions because they can fulfil not only ambitions with regard to economic value but also larger societal values is prominent throughout the text.

Rhenman also launches the 'business idea' concept, which is considered by many SIAR alumni to be the most emblematic concept of the group (see e.g. Carlsson, 2000). Interestingly, however, it is referred to in this book not as a 'business idea' but as 'systems for domination'. A system for domination is a system that includes a repertoire of interrelated assets, processes, norms and values that respond to changes in the environment. Here, Rhenman talks about three broad characteristics of systems for domination: (1) superior requisite variety (a reference to Ashby, 1956); (2) superior subsystems or components (a reference to Barnard's (1938) concept of 'strategic factors'); and (3) 'survival of the fittest', which perhaps can best be labelled the ability to change, or 'luck'.

Given these suggestions about 'systems for domination', one can deduce Rhenman's notion of a concept of the business idea (this is not difficult as it is described in rigorous detail in several subsequent SIAR publications). A business idea describes the match, or lack thereof, between the components of the external environment and those of the internal environment. It is quite obvious, as early as in this piece from 1969, that it is influenced not only by the likes of Selznick and Barnard but also by other, perhaps more typical strategy scholars, such as Chandler and the business policy researchers from Harvard. One other systemic concept that is integral to Rhenman's view of strategy is 'territory', by which he means the wider niche the company serves, the nature of the demands of that particular niche, and how thinking of business in terms of territories allows us to see not only threats but also opportunities for innovation and new business development. In addition, Rhenman reminds us of the fact that there are usually competitors around to disrupt things. Rhenman (1969a, pp. 123–4) writes: 'Repeatedly, we have felt an urge to remind corporate leaders that they are not alone on the market, that competitors are planning for the future too. Generally, they have agreed with us, . . . but seldom have our remarks had any real influence on the planning.'

Rhenman is not the first scholar to discuss strategy and come up with his own definition, and the 1969 book is not particularly clear with regard to his own definition. But he refers to Barnard (1938) and talks about 'meaningful' features and changes, mentioning 'change of market, change of owners and owner structure and the structure of the personnel' (Rhenman, 1969a, p. 126) as examples of strategic change. He suggests that 'it is our experience that the strategy often takes the character of general principles for the development of systems [business ideas]'. Scale and scope are important features of the systems.

While the last years of the 1960s flourished when it came to practical problem-solving and empirical input, Rhenman's academic output in the form of thought-provoking books and papers was diminishing, and partly taken over by junior associates. These included Bengt Stymne's (1970) thesis on organisation values, which extended our understanding of the business idea concept. Stymne had already been close to Rhenman as a student and accompanied him for many years. Stymne had also spent some time in the United States, where he became acquainted with Selznick's sociological take on organisation and strategy, thereby paralleling Rhenman's enthusiasm for Selznick's work. Stymne's PhD thesis was one of the more prominent examples of this sociological turn in SIAR's development. Stymne was one of many who had left SIAR by 1970, when the consulting operations had finally taken over academic research, and he carried on from the more academic side of management with an impressive catalogue of research on a broad set of matters. Stymne was also heavily involved in the formation and management of Fenix, a joint, collaborative research programme between industry partners and the SSE and Chalmers during the late 1990s and the early 2000s (more on this later).

Richard Normann

There were many other members of SIAR who produced scientific papers and theses, but, when it comes to scientific impact, two colleagues stood out: Rhenman and Richard Normann. Rhenman supervised Normann's PhD studies on organisational renewal and innovation. Normann defended his licentiate thesis in 1969, and published an article in the *Administrative Science Quarterly* (ASQ) (Normann, 1971), probably the most prestigious academic journal for publication of management research at the time. This was a major achievement by Swedish standards, although Normann's colleagues at SIAR were only moderately impressed (status came through problem resolution, not academic papers). As one of them said: 'The ASQ piece was just a fun distraction, there was no song and dance about it.'

Normann was originally interested in innovation, and used the business idea model to understand it. The ASQ piece (Normann, 1971) is positioned primarily in relation to the models by March and Simon (1958), Burns and Stalker (1961) and Lawrence and Lorsch (1967). It is based on thirteen case studies of innovation management in capital-intensive industries. Normann (1971) approaches innovation from the business idea perspective and claims that although innovation has to do with changes to the product, the product cannot be understood on its own; 'the organisation' and 'the environment' must be understood simultaneously, as a mutually interdependent complex of subsystems. *Consonance* is the key concept; it refers to the relations between the needs and values of the *market*, the properties of the *product*, and the task system, the cognitive system and the political system of the *organisation*. And in order to understand innovation, Normann (1971) argues, we must distinguish between product *variation* and *reorientation*. Apparently, this refinement of the concept of innovation was considered something of a novelty at the time. Anyway, Normann (1971) claims that in order to understand the challenges associated with different kinds of innovation, one needs to consider the whole system of organisation-internal and organisation-external features, and how they operate together. The general theory is that innovation requires a systematic and holistic approach to the possible consonance between firm, product and environment.

Normann (1975) defended his PhD thesis on growth (*Skapande Företagsledning [Creative Corporate Management]*) in 1975 and was immediately awarded his docentship, meaning that the thesis and his defence of it had such qualities that Normann was considered to have obtained habilitation directly. The thesis deals with processes of renewal and, conceptually and occasionally empirically, with growth in all its various forms. Normann positions his project in relation to Penrose (1959), Chandler (1962), Ansoff (1965) and different representatives of the contingency school (Burns & Stalker, 1961; Woodward, 1965; Lawrence & Lorsch, 1967). He also discusses Selznick (1957) and the importance of understanding the 'world of ideas' in organisations, as well as their historical origins. The overarching argument rests on a set of models. The business idea takes prominence as a more or less formal perspective on the matter that firms can work with to generate growth and drive renewal. Normann deals with the concept in relative depth. He also discusses changes to it, and means by which this can happen. Essentially, this includes anything imaginable in the form of management, including the non-linear matters that were perhaps under-studied at the time. It is logical that the thesis ends with the suggestion that in periods of change executive management should be viewed as statesmanship rather than 'mere' management; he wrote a monograph on this subject alone a year later (Normann, 1976).

At the same time, SIAR researchers slowly came to emphasise the fact that firms are different and that ideas cannot be generalised easily across industries. Rhenman had been interested in the management of hospitals in the past (Rhenman, 1969b) and now others took over (e.g. Svalander, 1979, 1982; Lind 1993). Service, the other 'industry', eventually became Normann's project. Normann was in charge of these studies and when he eventually left SIAR towards the end of the 1970s to settle in Paris and start up his own consulting operation, the Service Management Group (SMG), he had formed a framework for service businesses. These were published in 1984. The five main components of Normann's service management system were the service concept itself, the market segment, the delivery system and the image, all resting on the norms and values of the firm (Normann, 2001). The framework bears a strong resemblance to the business idea concept, with consonance as a major part. After Normann's departure, SIAR lost a lot of its edge when it came to service management.

Normann also continued to develop his research frameworks, helped in part by his remaining in academia; he was a visiting professor at Lund, Copenhagen Business School and Harvard Business School. Via service management, he came to focus on a range of matters such as innovation (and how incumbent markets were disrupted by 'invasions': *Invadörernas dans [The Dance of the Invaders]* (Normann, 1989)), customer interaction, value constellations, and knowledge and value creation. Normann and Ramirez (1993) criticise existing views on strategy, in particular the popular value-chain concept, as introduced by Porter (1985), as well as the predominant view that strategy can be planned. In a sense, Normann and Ramirez (1993) manage to criticise the added-value value-chain approach, the reliance on planning and the narrow outlook of our tools for strategic analysis, all the while suggesting a big picture (systemic) approach involving far more instances than the firm and its existing customer base: 'successful companies conceive of strategy as systematic social innovation: the continuous design and redesign of complex business systems' (Normann and Ramirez, 1993, p. 66).

Normann's project on the service sector put him in a new strategy context: strategy as something centred on the relation to and interaction with the customer, including the ecosystems, if you will, surrounding that interaction. These ideas were further developed in a subsequent piece, *Knowledge and Value*, by Wikström and Normann (1994), although with a stronger focus on the cognitive processes that go on in interactions. The different interfaces of the value constellations of a firm are places where knowledge is exchanged and value created. Normann did not publish much after this. He passed away in 2003, having published his last book in 2001; *Reframing Business* (Normann, 2001) is at the same time an analytical summary of his own legacy, a smooth positioning of it in relation to main characters in business studies and philosophy, and an application of his broader framework on contemporary management challenges.

The Demise of Scientific SIAR

By around 1970, SIAR leaders had definitely accepted that the large projects they took on were more or less impossible to run through the bureaucratic university system. In our interviews with SIAR alumni, they all make suggestions along the lines that 'we weren't really interested in writing papers and stuff; we wanted to solve problems'. Many SIAR associates had part-time jobs in academia and continued to publish thought pieces and the like. This gradual shift culminated in what SIAR alumni refer to as the 'culture revolution' in 1970, after which thirteen members of staff, including several of the founders, left SIAR to pursue university careers.

For those who stayed, a logic emerged that explained how consultancy and academic research could be combined. The SIAR approach, or narrative, would be that SIAR was doing 'clinical research'. The metaphor at hand was the surgeon operating on the patient, in front of others, in the theatre, applying theory. This was also a successful learning strategy. According to Lind and Rhenman (1989), it appeared that those members of staff who focused more on consulting than on research learned more, and that the actual resolving of problems opened up for more advanced learnings. As Lind and Rhenman (1989, p. 167) wrote:

> The consultants in the institute who concentrated on consulting seemed to be learning more and developing more knowledge than those mainly involved in research. Traditional field research seemed to be useful to a certain kind of exploration, but real theoretical breakthrough seemed to come out of in-depth consultative work with a few organisations, or, often and best of all, with one.

Throughout the 1970s, SIAR staff continued to churn out academic papers, theses and internally published memos and books. The 1970s had seen a much stronger focus on consulting, but the academic character of the firm remained, as SIAR was known to be something of the 'reflective client's alternative', a research-based consulting firm. Today, the legacy of SIAR, at Swedish and foreign universities and among consulting firms and clients, is thin. Since SIAR researchers typically published their more important pieces in Swedish and in their internal publishing outlet, the global audience had no opportunity to read them, with some exceptions. Those researchers did, of course, have an impact via publications, including textbook publications such as Bruzelius and Skärvad (1974), in addition to consulting, and, we must remember, as teachers of generations of business students.

3.2.2 Internationalisation at Uppsala and the SSE

Uppsala and Sune Carlson

Uppsala and Lund were the first universities to form business administration departments, in 1958. Nils Västhagen, who was geared more towards accounting, was appointed to the chair in Lund, and Sune Carlson to the chair in Uppsala. Carlson had received his PhD in economics in the 1930s and then worked for the United Nations (UN) in New York for the better part of the 1950s. Carlson had been influenced by the likes of Barnard and was also keen on method matters, meaning his first pieces were heavily centred on the daily work of managers (on which more later). Soon, however, Carlson would broaden his horizons significantly. Returning from his work for the UN, Carlson took up his position at Uppsala University, where he opted not to continue his studies of top executives but instead initiated studies of firms' internationalisation processes.

The international business research programme was established at the beginning of the 1960s and included empirical research on Swedish multinationals and their internationalisation processes and strategies. The programme collected data from more than 2,000 subsidiaries through a questionnaire directed to Swedish multinationals in 1964 and 1969–70 (Welch et al., 2016). Vahlne and Wiedersheim-Paul (1973) and Carlson (1975) have summarised the results of this research programme. Carlson's empirical studies of internationalisation departed from the main assumptions that managers typically lack knowledge of foreign markets and operations and that this knowledge can be obtained only through operations abroad, that is, through experiential learning. He first formulated the proposition that firms tend to handle risky problems by trial and error and by gradually learning about foreign markets: 'Once the firm has passed the cultural barriers and had its first experience of foreign operations, it is generally willing to conquer one market after another' (Carlson, 1966,

p. 15). Overall, Carlson took a rather sceptical view of managers and their ability to lead firms based on superior knowledge. In his book *Executive Behavior*, he writes (Carlson, 1951, p. 52): 'Before we made the study, I always thought of a chief executive as the conductor of an orchestra, standing aloof on his platform. Now I am in some respects inclined to see him as the puppet in a puppet show with hundreds of people pulling the strings and forcing him to act in one way or another.'

However, it was primarily not Carlson who became associated with the Uppsala school of internationalisation but his doctoral students Jan Johanson, Jan-Erik Vahlne and Finn Wiedersheim-Paul. The most cited paper is the Johanson and Vahlne (1977) one published in the *Journal of International Business Studies* and based on case studies of four Swedish multinationals and their subsidiaries' internationalisation processes. It is here that they introduce the two main components of the Uppsala model of the internationalisation process: first, a progressive establishment of a chain of operations starting with direct export to subsidiaries; and second, selection of markets to enter based on physical distance from the home market; that is, firms begin entering markets that are geographically and culturally close to the home market and then enter more distant markets later. The model has been somewhat revised (Johanson & Vahlne, 1990, 2009), but overall has remained remarkably stable. The Uppsala model portrays a slow and risk-minimising internationalisation that supports moving forward only when the internationalisation process results in positive learning feedback. Many researchers have accused the model of excluding the possibility of more strategic internationalisation processes, in particular studies of 'born globals' (e.g. Bengtsson, 2004), by which is meant small firms that internationalise very early through selecting large markets before neighbouring small ones and committing heavily to the foreign market from the beginning. However, the Uppsala model has repeatedly been shown, in empirical studies, to depict the most common ways of internationalising (Johanson & Vahlne, 2009).

In terms of the strategy aspect of internationalisation strategies, the Uppsala model has always been rather silent. 'Basically, the process model is rather sceptical in regard to strategy', according to Johanson and Vahlne (1990, p. 22). The scepticism towards strategy is rooted in the view of internationalisation as a trial-and-error learning process for individual managers within an organisation of loosely coupled systems providing few possibilities to make that learning organisational. Thus, the Uppsala model sees internationalisation more as an emergent strategy following certain patterns, rather than a planned strategy. However, considering the way strategists define strategy (e.g. Mintzberg, 1978), the view of Johanson and Vahlne by no means excludes it from being conceived of as potentially integral to strategy. The Uppsala model emerged as a result of many different projects on internationalisation processes at Uppsala (Vahlne, 2020). Several researchers were involved, and according to Vahlne (2020) the core article from 1977 was based on inductive work, albeit guided by general business theory, such as Penrose (1959) and Cyert and March (1963).

The business administration department at Uppsala University continues to be the leading institution in Sweden for research on multinational corporation (MNC) strategy. Some twenty researchers, including doctoral students, are actively researching internationalisation processes and management of MNCs, producing a steady stream of dissertations and quality publications in the area. One of the leading international textbooks on MNCs comes from here (Forsgren, 2017) and perhaps the internal rivalry between international process researchers and MNC researchers in the department (see Forsgren, 2016, for another recent critique of the Uppsala model) has helped them remain internationally competitive in the MNC strategy research domain. It is somewhat striking that Uppsala has maintained such a strong presence in one subject field for more than four decades (at the time of writing, the Johanson and Vahlne article from 1977 has been cited more than 17,000 times according to Google Scholar, which represents a highly respectable impact by Swedish social science standards). Internationalisation researchers at Uppsala (probably) think of themselves not as strategy researchers but as students of internationalisation and globalisation processes, period. For a strategy researcher, as suggested, there is no problem in conceiving of it as a subset of the strategy subject field.

SSE: The Institute of International Business

Management research at the SSE had a relatively late start, given how long it had been around.[6] As the name indicates, it had been, since its inception in 1909, a school primarily orientated towards economics in education and research, with Eli Heckscher and Bertil Ohlin the most renowned economics researchers. They studied international trade and formulated the Hecksher–Ohlin theorem, namely that capital-abundant countries will primarily export capital-intensive goods and labour-abundant countries will primarily export labour-intensive goods. Many alumni and associates from the SSE ended up elsewhere as the main universities set up new departments for business studies. Eric Rhenman went to Lund, Sune Carlsson ended up in Uppsala, to mention but two.

In the mid-1970s a new line of strategy research started at the SSE with the formation of the Institute of International Business (IIB). In the subject area of economics, the SSE was renowned primarily for its research on international

---

[6] *This section builds on Rehnberg (2009), unless otherwise stated.*

trade. International trade and business come naturally to both practitioners and researchers of economics and management in Sweden. A small, open economy provides strong incentives for growing companies to do international business. A donation by Swedish industrialists made it possible to start the IIB research institute in 1976, with a focus on MNC strategies. The IIB is a cornerstone in the strategy research undertaken at the SSE. The leading strategy researchers at the IIB have been Gunnar Hedlund, Örjan Sölvell and Udo Zander.

Hedlund received his doctorate in 1976 with the dissertation *The Multinational Corporation, the State and the Trade Unions* (Hedlund, 1976). This was a typical topic at that time in Sweden, that is, how the MNC, the state and the trade unions could coexist and work together in a more internationalised world. In 1980, Hedlund became the director of the IIB and his research became more focused on the strategic and organisational problems of large MNCs. During this time, the SSE's research was orientated more towards the strategic management of MNCs, while the other influential group of researchers in international business at Uppsala focused more on companies' internationalisation processes (e.g. Johanson and Vahlne, 1977).

The most influential of Hedlund's research projects concerned the MNC and the strategic and organisational principle of heterarchy, also called the N-Form. Inspired by Nonaka's writings on knowledge creation in Japanese firms and the SECI (socialisation, externalisation, combination, internalisation) process (Nonaka, 1994), as well as working together with Nonaka (Hedlund & Nonaka, 1993), Hedlund proposed the N-Form as a more effective organisation for knowledge creation and transformation than the M-Form (Chandler, 1977; Williamson, 1985). Hedlund (1986, 1994). He argued that the M-Form organisation (the divisional hierarchy), so commonly used by large MNCs in the Western world, divides knowledge into divisions, and is based on permanent structures and vertical communication, making top management critical for creating new knowledge combinations. The aim of new knowledge combinations is to create semi-independent parts (new divisions), diversifying the corporation further. In contrast, the N-Form (the heterarchy) works with temporary structures and lateral communication, allowing for knowledge combinations at lower and middle levels of the organisation. The aim is to focus the corporation on rich fields of knowledge elements that can be combined. Hedlund's point was that the N-Form is a much more effective organisation form for knowledge creation and transformation than the M-Form. Hedlund's argument for the superiority of the N-Form is nicely illustrated by Prahalad and Hamel's (1990) concept of the corporation's core competence. They advocate for the competitive advantage of organising for knowledge combinations and identify the M-Form as an obstacle to building core competencies. Hedlund was a pioneer in Swedish strategy research in that he introduced knowledge management as a sub-field of strategy and international business research.

The formation of the IIB offered a governance structure with possibly greater leeway for academic unorthodoxy. Paired with the support of industry through donations and empirical proximity (Tetra Pak, Ericsson and the Wallenberg sphere were among the founders), the IIB researchers had fantastic opportunities to study MNC structure and control, which resulted in significant work on said questions. In that sense, the IIB had an approach not unlike that of SIAR, with the aim not only to improve Swedish research on international business but also to help firms. Unfortunately, Hedlund died in 1996, aged just forty-nine. Two of Hedlund's former doctoral students, Örjan Sölvell and Udo Zander, continued the highly influential strategy research at the IIB, in the 1990s and at the beginning of the 2000s. Their work will be described in more detail in Section 3.3.3. The IIB was terminated in the late 2000s and integrated with the marketing and strategy sections of the SSE.

3.2.3 Process-Orientated Research

Several, perhaps a majority of, strategy researchers in Sweden have been applying a process perspective since strategy research started. In the early era, one could find it in most places but perhaps primarily in Gothenburg, Linköping and, to a lesser extent, at the SSE. In the following we touch base with the works of Carlson, Ulf af Trolle, Bo Hedberg, Melin, Jan Wallander and others.

Sune Carlson's Work on Management Behaviour

As described in the earlier section 'Uppsala and Sune Carlson', Carlson gained his PhD from the SSE in the 1930s, and before departing for New York, and later Uppsala, he conducted research on management, in particular the behaviour of top managers. His most influential publication, the book *Executive Behavior* (Carlson, 1951), reported the results from a study of the day-to-day work of nine top executives in nine large Swedish companies. Carlson found that top managers' work tends to be very reactive in response to external events and actors and that the top managers seldom found the time to reflect on actions so as to initiate more strategic and proactive ones. In short, they were not the strategic and rational decision-makers that Carlson had expected them to be. The study received much attention within management research and inspired several international researchers to undertake similar studies; among these was Henry Mintzberg's (1973) dissertation *The Nature of Managerial Work*.

Carlson proposed that future management studies should focus on the deviations from theoretically efficient management methods and how to overcome them. Carlson's account of management behaviour was sometimes detailed when it came to method discussion and also in his descriptions of management. One observation was the importance of geography (Tengblad, 2003). Carlson had noticed that the physical location and layout of the head office affected the CEO's communication pattern, in both external and internal contacts. For example, he observed that managers whose offices were in the same building but on a different floor had much less contact with the CEO than managers who were on the same floor. The effect was even greater for managers located in other, more distant buildings. He actually advised one of the CEOs he studied to rotate the physical location of the managers so that the managers responsible for the most pressing issues at any one time were closer to the CEO's office, and others with less need for contact were farther away (Tengblad, 2003).

However, upon returning to Uppsala as the new chair in business administration, Carlson discontinued the corporate behaviour management research agenda to focus on internationalisation processes (see the earlier section 'Uppsala and Sune Carson'). At the SSE, these types of behavioural studies of top managers were largely abandoned until they were resumed by Sven-Erik Sjöstrand (e.g. 1997) and others, albeit from an organisational and institutional theory perspective. It is perhaps noteworthy that Carlson changed the direction of his research to what might be considered the direct opposite of mundane everyday management work: big picture questions in the big world. But this mirrored the changes in society and in Sweden very well. At the time of his return to Sweden and Uppsala, the international arena for business was radically different from what it had been when he had conducted his behaviour studies in the 1940s. The behaviour studies were conducted in close proximity to Carlson's contacts in the business world, and even those that took place in a time when the overlap between academia and industry was substantial came across as highly rigorous; as mentioned elsewhere in this Element, Carlson's (1951) account of methodology and the applied methods is meticulous (and extensive) and can be interpreted as a way to justify research on managers and to establish a business studies discipline.

The Gothenburg School of Strategy Formation

One prominent business administration researcher in the early days was Ulf af Trolle, a professor at Gothenburg between 1951 and 1967. Very much a man of his time, af Trolle had expertise in many areas, even though his main field was distribution, marketing and sales. He believed in the combination of theory and practice and worked closely with firms and industry. He was also a prominent figure in the public debate on firms, industry and policy. Like others, he wrote primarily in Swedish for a Swedish audience, and little of his academic legacy has a bearing today. But af Trolle influenced many students who later became CEOs, as well as economic and trade policies in the 1950s and 1960s. He also initiated the Institute for Advanced Marketing (IHM), aimed at educating sales and marketing people, which has been very successful in attracting talent in Sweden.

Camping on Seesaws

As indicated, strategy has not necessarily been a distinct subject field in all business administration departments in Sweden; this was the case in both Uppsala and Gothenburg. This did not, however, stop scholars at these institutions from considering themselves, or being considered by others, to be strategy researchers. Bo Hedberg is one such researcher. He gained his PhD from Gothenburg University in 1971 and became a docent in 1972, and was one of the more important Swedish writers on strategy, particularly during the 1970s. Hedberg was a child of his time and, like other young scholars, greatly influenced by the Carnegie Mellon tradition. Like his contemporary Richard Normann, he also used much of the thinking of the contingency school (e.g. Burns & Stalker, 1961; Lawrence & Lorsch, 1967). However, whereas Normann and other SIAR-ites had slipped over to the more sociological approach of Selznick, Hedberg was also influenced by Karl Weick.

Another characteristic of Hedberg, like many of his contemporaries, was his interest in practical matters. As early as 1977, he became a professor at the *Arbetslivscentrum* [Centre for Swedish Working Life], a government-sponsored institute for research on all matters relating to work, and remained in that position until the mid-1980s when he shifted career to become a C-suite executive at the Swedish Savings Banks Association. He continued there until the early 1990s, when he was appointed to a chair at Stockholm University; at the same time, he joined Cepro, a successful Swedish management consulting firm. Whereas Hedberg's main scientific legacy clearly came out of the productive 1970s, he continued to publish important work while a practitioner in the latter half of the 1980s and 1990s. In 2000, Hedberg suffered a stroke and never really came back as a researcher or a consultant. He passed away in 2012.

Hedberg also had a very eclectic approach to business administration. Like many others in those days, he was not restricted by subject fields but wrote about many different aspects, such as corporate democracy (Hedberg et al., 1972), information systems (e.g. Hedberg et al., 1976), computerisation (e.g. Hedberg et al., 1975), industrial politics (e.g. Hedberg & Sjöstrand, 1979) and more. But Hedberg's main contribution, at least initially, was his work on firms in crisis or in stagnant environments, and their struggle to change (or their complete lack of capacity to change). Hedberg himself might not have phrased it this way, but with today's nomenclature he would have clearly been termed a *strategy process* researcher. He would later (Hedberg & Jönsson, 1989) label the research that he and his colleagues were doing 'the Gothenburg school on strategy formation', with a focus on factors behind strategic change and the role of 'myths' (perhaps best defined as 'worldviews'), 'reality' and the alignment between the two.

Hedberg is probably best known for his ASQ piece *Camping on Seesaws: Prescriptions for a Self-Designing Organization*, which he co-wrote with Paul Nystrom and Bill Starbuck in 1976 (Hedberg et al., 1976). Here, the focus is on how to create autonomous organisations or organisations capable of changing. The metaphors of 'tent' and 'palace' are fundamental, and the authors suggest that organisations need to erect tents as tents allow for greater flexibility (Hedberg et al., 1976, p. 45): 'An organizational tent places greater emphasis on flexibility, creativity, immediacy, and initiative than on authority, clarity, decisiveness, or responsiveness; and an organizational tent neither asks for harmony between the activities of different organizational components, nor asks that today's behavior resemble yesterday's or tomorrow's. Why behave more consistently than one's world does?'

Hedberg and colleagues (1976) take us through the stages of stagnation and the conditions under which organisations can avoid going under, instead turning from a state of crisis onto a path of survival. In line with perceiving themselves as tents, organisations need to design processes in a way that balances six so-called fulcra – consensus, contentment, affluence, faith, consistency and rationality (in decision-making and planning) – in a philosophy that assumes that everything is U-shaped. Hedberg and colleagues (1976) frequently refer to well-known contingency scholars such as Thompson, 1967, and Galbraith, 1973, as well as to younger scholars such as Normann, 1971, and Miller and Mintzberg, 1974, and the article follows in a stream of research concerned with organisational and strategic change that is typical for the time. It is perhaps also emblematic for the time period in the sense that it is written in a very normative, prescriptive way (even the title supports this observation). These are younger researchers keen on using the tools and the concepts of their relatively newborn subject field to improve things in organisations. Furthermore, like much other literature from the same period, the style of writing is relatively free of detailed talk of data. Instead, the text, packed with metaphors ('tents', 'palaces', 'accelerators', 'decelerators', 'stabilisers' etc.), takes an overarching perspective and talks of strategy and management from a high level, with a certain degree of confidence – a confidence that comes from close proximity to the objects of study and a deep understanding of how things worked (or not) in organisations.

Myth and Reality

Together with those who represented what became known as the Strategy School of Gothenburg, namely Sten Jönsson, Lennart Sjöberg, Rolf Lundin (all of whom had chairs in fields other than strategy) and Nils Brunsson (who was in Gothenburg at the time), Hedberg continued to write about change. He did this from numerous angles, although his ideas as a young scholar prevailed for a long time. In the early part of the 1970s he studied industries (e.g. steel) and firms (e.g. Facit, a mechanical office machines supplier famous for its inability to meet the competition from Japanese providers of electronic solutions), which appeared to lay the foundation for the theories and approaches that he and others from Gothenburg later came to launch. In Hedberg and Jönsson (1977), the authors outline their perspective on strategy formulation, suggesting that strategies are the rules operationalised from 'dominant myths'. Thus, strategies are the detailed features of the myths of the firm. Strategies mediate between myth and reality, the objective world 'out there'. Strategy is the rules that govern the relationship between objective reality and subjective reality, as perceived by the organisation. And, in that logic, strategy formulation is often a continuous, incremental process, where myth and reality are sufficiently aligned. However, when there is a mismatch, the organisation is either in crisis or heading towards it, and strategic change (formulation) is imperative. Firms that have been successful for a long time have a tendency to build excessive *inertia* and insensitivity to external changes. In such cases, myths and strategies are very strong and when existing myths are finally perceived as dysfunctional it can be very difficult to create new myths. Firms need some form of myth change in order to change strategy, and such a change of myths typically comes from the perception of a crisis.

The Hedberg and Jönsson (1977) piece is something of a white paper for the Gothenburg school. Hedberg and Jönsson (and others) used concepts such as 'inertia' and 'unlearning' and described in some detail the difficulties with which myths were replaced. Hedberg later returned to the concept of inertia, in Hedberg and Ericson (1979); there, they discuss 'insight inertia' and 'action inertia' – probably the model that Hedberg is most well-known for, at least in Sweden.

Much later, in 1989, Hedberg and Jönsson (1989) wrote a summary and retrospective article on the strategy research at Gothenburg in the 1970s; although much is repetition from the 1977 piece, they also add new takes on their historical work, for example the need to shift myths rather swiftly at the time, in order to avoid prolonged periods of uncertainty. The article also discusses the growing dynamics of the modern world of organisations, and our propensity to change things very often, perhaps too often.

Hedberg continued his career both in practical contexts and also, from 1990 onwards, as a professor at Stockholm University. Perhaps his most notable publication was the book *Imaginära Organisationer [Imaginary Organisations]* (Hedberg, 1994), which outlined a new perspective on organisations. Hedberg had worked a a great deal with computerisation and management information systems (MIS) (e.g. Hedberg, 1971; Hedberg & Jönsson, 1978), from a strategy perspective, and this project built on Hedberg's broad repertoire. Describing imaginary organisations, Hedberg (1994) referred to those kinds of systems and constellations of multiple organisations that today we might call 'ecosystems', 'constellations', 'network organisations' or 'clusters'; firms that share resources, platforms, information systems, processes and more, without being part of the same legal entity. The main enabler here, naturally, is the development of information and communication technologies. *Imaginära Organisationer* (Hedberg, 1994) had a significant impact on research at the turn of the millennium, but perhaps even more of an impact on practice. The model was used by numerous organisations, not least the clients at Cepro, where Hedberg was a consultant.

Linköping

One of the most prominent strategy scholars in Sweden is Leif Melin, who has a broad repertoire of research stretching from the 1970s. Melin is also something of a figurehead in relation to the international community and has been a member of the SMS since its early days. Melin co-organised the SMS conference in Stockholm in 1990. He was a pioneer at Linköping but later moved to Jönköping International Business School, which accentuated his turn towards entrepreneurship.

Melin originally studied purchasing strategies and organisation in his dissertation (Melin, 1977), inspired by the Industrial Marketing and Purchasing (IMP) Group's network approach.[7] It was the first dissertation in business studies from Linköping, which had recently received university status. At the end of the 1970s and the beginning of the 1980s, Sweden's economy took a severe downturn after having seen more or less continuous growth and expansion from the early 1950s. After his dissertation, Melin became involved in a large research project that studied the decline of the city of Motala, a traditional industrial city

---

[7] *The IMP Group consists of European universities researching relational and interaction issues in industrial contexts.*

not far from Linköping, and how the companies, the public sector and the trade unions were responding to this decline. Among the companies in Motala facing decline was a major Swedish consumer electronics company, Luxor, that manufactured colour televisions. This case study became part of a larger study of how six Scandinavian colour TV manufacturers responded strategically to the declining market in the early 1980s (Melin, 1985). In this paper, Melin introduces his field-of-force model, which describes and analyses the external and internal forces affecting the focal firm and the collaborative relationships with its suppliers and customers. The field-of-force model is clearly inspired by the IMP Group's (in relation to which Melin had written his thesis) network approach and as such represents a more collaborative than competitive view (e.g. Porter, 1980) of an industry and its dynamics. Melin (1987, 1989) further develops his thinking about the field-of-force model and stresses the importance of understanding external, strategic and internal forces simultaneously, and how they interplay, in order to understand strategic changes of the firm and its networks.

At the time, strategy research had become increasingly occupied with more atomistic and reductionist ways of researching and explaining strategic change, a development Melin clearly disliked. With Melin being a strategy process and change researcher, it was natural that he contribute to a special issue of the SMJ concerning strategy process, with a review of research of internationalisation as a strategy process (Melin, 1992). Melin identifies three research streams: stage models of internationalisation (with the Uppsala process model as a large contributor); the strategy, structure and control of the MNC (with the SSE as a large contributor); and the process school of international management. So, perhaps the most characteristic feature of Melin's work is his focus on process, be it change and turnaround in general terms or internationalisation processes. Although Melin has a broad production list, including family business, general entrepreneurship, leadership and strategising, one common denominator is process – so much so that he later became one of the leading proponents of the strategy-as-practice perspective. We will return to this later.

In 1995 Melin moved from Linköping to Jönköping when he received a chair in strategy and organisation, with an emphasis on family business strategy, at the then newly established university. Jönköping International Business School is located in a region of southern Sweden that is renowned for its entrepreneurship, with a strong representation of small and medium-sized enterprises (SMEs), many of which are family firms. Most of Melin's research after the turn of the millennium has concerned strategy process issues related to family firms. In 2005 he founded, together with colleagues, a research institute at Jönköping University, the Centre for Family Enterprise and Ownership

(CeFEO). This has since become a leading research centre focusing on family firms; it is ranked no. 1 in Europe and no. 6 in the world, based on publications in the research area. In addition, Melin has contributed to a common strategic issue for most family firms, the issue of the succession of ownership (Sund et al., 2015). The business studies department at Jönköping University is today the leading institution in Sweden for strategy research related to SMEs and family firms, to a large extent owing to Melin's efforts to organise this research. As stated, his contribution to the strategy-as-practice field will be discussed in Section 3.3.4.

Jan Wallander – Reflective Practitioner

Stockholm University and its department of business administration is a younger creature and did not reach prominence primarily through strategy in the early days. One very important Swedish management thinker came from Stockholm University and the field of economics. Jan Wallander is perhaps known primarily not for his academic research but rather for his deeds as a business person, and a very reflective such. Wallander is also a striking example of the ease with which people moved between academia and industry. As CEO of Svenska Handelsbanken (a major Swedish bank) between 1970 and 1978 he was extremely successful; he is often described as one of the most successful Swedish CEOs of all time. Wallander was a doctor and a docent (and an acting professor) of economics (albeit specialising in typical business administration issues) from Stockholm University. He was the head of *Industrins Utredningsinstitut* (IUI, a national industrial think tank and research centre) when, aged forty-one, he switched industry entirely and took over as CEO of Sundsvallsbanken. Sundsvallsbanken was a regional bank in the north of Sweden whose main area of interest was the forestry industry. However, during Wallander's time at the bank, it became hugely successful and competitive on a national level.

Wallander rose to fame for his many bold strategic moves, and later in life he would publish these experiences. Among other things, he was highly critical of the use of budgets and received widespread attention when he abandoned this in the bank almost immediately after assuming the position as CEO. This was something that also generated fame among management scholars. One of the reasons why he saw budgets as an 'unnecessary evil' was probably his background at IUI, which among other things worked with forecasts, and where Wallander had learned that the major and most interesting shifts were not often detected or foreseen in forecasts and regular budgets (e.g. Hope & Fraser, 2003).

Wallander was also a firm believer in decentralisation and in pushing responsibility out as close as possible to the market; he created a network of

autonomous bank branches (close to the upmarket clients the bank was target-
ing). Wallander also established a highly successful profit-sharing scheme,
Oktogonen, which was contingent upon relative performance vis-à-vis competitors. Here it should be noted that Svenska Handelsbanken has constantly
exceeded the average of its competition since the scheme was implemented.
A consequence of this is that the largest shareholder of the bank has long been
the personnel foundation, meaning that the bank is to a certain extent personnel-
owned. The creation of *Oktogonen* also gave the bank's personnel shares and
real influence through board representation, as well as hefty financial pension
rewards; at times, every member of staff with more than twenty years of service
received at least SEK 10 million (roughly EUR 1 million) upon retirement. The
Oktogonen set-up has been hailed from many angles, but it was a clear testament
to Wallander's ideas of real incentives, decentralisation, motivation and com-
mitment. Which worked, arguably. Many others have tried to mimic the
Handelsbanken strategy, with varying results.

Wallander is perhaps a strange character from a contemporary perspective. At
the same time, his entire career signals that management was perhaps slightly
different in those days in Sweden. A professor could be in demand for major
jobs in industry, such as CEO, and a professor's thoughts on management could
make a major difference when turned into practice. There were no silos in place,
and the two subcultures were not framed very far away from each other.

3.2.4 End of an Era

In Section 3.2, then, we have described some of the more important contributions and contributors from what we refer to as the earlier period of Swedish
strategy research. We have argued throughout the Element that this period is
characterised by systemic, all-encompassing models, an interest in internationalisation and a process-orientated approach. These contributions are also
almost exclusively qualitative in nature and take the perspective that business
is controllable and that the role of students is to help improve business. Many of
these models are unique in relation to, say, their American contemporaries. The
research described here, from the early era, all had a great impact by Swedish
standards, theoretically and methodologically. There is no exact point in time
when we leave the old and enter the new, but, as we have stated throughout this
Element, sometime in the late 1980s and after 1990, research moves from
having a very national touch, based on Swedish experiences, to an international, or American, epistemology. Some features remain, such as the qualitative approach, the process orientation and the continued study of
internationalisation. Others, like the systemic approach, gradually start to

fade in favour of more variable-centred research questions. The view that business is controllable also partly disappears. Most importantly, however, the status of relevance and the will to help out and improve matters, which has hitherto been dominant, more or less vanish among academics (at least as long as academics were in academic milieus), in favour of rigour.

So, what distinguished the early era, with its optimistic agenda that hosted both a will to progress academically and, perhaps even more so, a will to help managers and companies out? We argue that a series of events helped steer the work of strategy researchers in a different direction: (1) the emergence of a competitive consulting industry; (2) the establishment of a global research society, most notably the formation of the SMS; (3) substantial changes to the organisation of Swedish universities; and (4) the relative isomorphism of global companies, using the same global logics and methods.

The Consultancy Market

The SIAR and other researchers we have described so far in this Element all had the opportunity to be both academics and consultants simultaneously. In the 1950s, 1960s and 1970s, managers had nowhere else to go but to the universities, which is where the collective scientific competence was. Few, if any, major consulting firms existed in the Swedish market and so the academics that so wanted could easily take on the dual role. Over time, however, both research and consultancy became global and competitive, leading inevitably to specialisation. Boston Consulting Group and later McKinsey entered the (non-competitive and lucrative) Swedish market in the 1980s and were followed by foreign and domestic competitors. In the 1990s, many of these consultants also initiated research institutes that in many ways catered for the knowledge that had hitherto been a monopoly for the academics.

This meant that many of the more academically geared consultants or academics-turned-advisors, such as SIAR, lost their strong position. In a way, the academic consultants gave up or lost their foothold, thereby speeding up the loss of relevance. One should also bear in mind that many researchers, particularly those more senior, continued to operate as consultants on their own or at one of the bigger consulting firms. But it was generally a divided operation, with limited, if any, overlap between consulting and empirical work on the one hand and academic research and publishing on the other. Few new SIAR-like institutes were created, and the character of the research output moved from prescriptive to descriptive. While research progressed, some would continue to publish *and* act as consultants, but rarely in the same projects, which had been the case earlier. We see several examples of successful researchers who managed to run successful consulting operations, but they did so outside of their university work.

Another contributing factor was probably the sheer fact that many of the young researchers that had started as PhD students in their twenties had now become middle-aged. They had their PhD degrees, their associate and full professorships, and now also the possibility to take on larger but unadulterated consulting jobs, which meant greater economic rewards than life in the department corridors (Andrésen et al., 2012).

A Global Research Society

As a parallel to the formation of a consulting industry, the scientific field became more integrated, to use Whitley's (1984) terminology. The national imprints, for lack of a better word, slowly faded away during the late 1980s and early 1990s. Research questions became more global, and individual institutions became more similar. Perhaps the 1980s was the decade when the field experienced something of a renaissance after the 1970s: the strategy field was dominated by practical models and ideas coming out of consulting firms such as McKinsey (e.g. portfolio analysis) and the Boston Consulting Group (e.g. the matrix, the learning curve), with Mintzberg one important exception.

Porter's (1980) Five Forces model gave the field the opportunity to enjoy the scientific shine and robustness of industrial organisation and micro-economics, and researchers were able to use the models to understand industry and firm performance. Unsurprisingly, the field, in actually having something, a fundamental theory of performance and competition, to gather around and talk about, spurred criticism and alternative takes, as a good disciplinary field should. And so both the process view (e.g. Mintzberg, 1978; also Bower, 1970; Burgelman, 1983, 1988; Chakravarthy and Doz, 1992; and more) and the resource-based view (RBV) (Barney, 1986, 1991) grew strong, as we now had something to relate to (and often position against). Rumelt and colleagues' (1994) book on the fundamental research issues is another good example of declarative texts that many could relate to and discuss. The field came alive, so to speak, which we argue further encouraged a more academic conversation on the matter of strategy, again in favour of rigour rather than relevance (it was not really a debate about, say, whether decision-makers preferred the Five Forces or the so-called VRIO (Valuable, Rare, Inimitable, Organised) framework for analytical support). Since then, the field has been further enriched with different models and theories of economics, including institutional theories and behavioural economics, all helping to drive rigour but not necessarily relevance.

Among the field-internal forces, one cannot neglect the widespread power of the SMS and its SMJ and annual conference, which were a key factor in the forming of a research community around a relatively uniform methodological agenda. The conference initially also drew an audience from business and consulting (the SMS annual conference was often referred to as an ABC conference, as it attracted Academics, Business people and Consultants, something which perhaps still happens, albeit not to the extent it once did). Nowadays it is a conference *for* academics arranged *by* academics. The conferences were also fertile ground for making international contacts. The Academy of Management, with its strategic management division, has also been important for the formation of a global society. Given that the stated ambition of the SMS was effectively to make the field more scientifically robust (and less like the case-centred approach of the Harvard Business School), it is not surprising that the focus of the field moved away from prescriptive models, practice proximity, cases and the every-day challenges that strategising managers face. The huge success of the SMS has been the deciding factor behind the establishment of the field, although it may not have helped move research closer to practice, as this never appeared to be the intention. Another consequence, important for many Swedish researchers, was the strong emphasis on hard science and quantitative approaches, which inevitably meant a greater focus on variables, which were typically studied out of context and only individually in relation to a possible dependent variable such as profit margin. This meant, for instance, that the sometimes clumsy, multifaceted models that most Swedes worked with (compare with the stakeholder model and the business idea concept) were harder to launch internationally.

The decision by the SMS to hold its tenth conference in Stockholm in 1990 is undoubtedly a very important milestone in the history of Swedish strategy research. Co-organised by Leif Melin of Linköping and Jönköping, and aimed at discussing the challenges of the 1990s, the conference was an indication that Swedes were a force to be reckoned with and were now part of the global strategy community. The participants included, among others, Michael Porter. For many Swedes, the conference also underlined that strategy was a research discipline in its own right, not simply a category of management problems. Many of the Swedish strategy researchers who were present testify to the event's importance in inspiring their research and in their becoming part of the global community.

Swedish University Reform

However, the Swedish education and research policy system also played a part in the shift of direction. Overall, the 1993 reform was intended to drive the quality of education and research and to render them more competitive, domestically as well as internationally. Overall funding was not reduced but would be distributed more competitively, based on performance. One central idea was to free universities from state and government intervention, which meant decentralisation and allowing universities to act more independently (Dahlqvist et al., 2019). Paired with this decentralisation were, among other things, new ways of funding research. Whereas a greater proportion of research grants historically came through the internal university channels, after the reform a fair share came through competitive calls from new national research foundations that were formed to administer the grant application systems. Between the early 1980s and the early 2000s, the external share of research grants grew from roughly one-third to two-thirds (Högskoleverket [Swedish Council for Higher Education], 2006). This meant, among other things, that senior researchers had to spend far more time writing up grant applications. We also argue that this drove rigour rather than anything else, as the application criteria were ultimately grounded in scientific merit only, which implied international publication. The change of funding was coupled with increased support for PhD students (an area that had been under scrutiny for a certain period of time, not least as PhD studies had been considered uncertain, difficult and generally underfunded on the part of the student) and not for senior researchers, which further meant that focus was on educating good scientists, not necessarily on relevance and the work of senior professors. Although Swedish PhD dissertations were traditionally written monographs, as in the faculties of law, social science, the arts and theology, the new era opened up for paper-based compilation theses, which had previously been the norm at faculties such as medicine, science and engineering. This meant that PhD students, almost from the start, had to decide on publication strategies and adhere to the standards of the international community. The features of the reform that related to research were not met with much resistance from the sector itself.

Apart from these institutional changes to the entire system, several organisational and cultural changes happened within the field of business administration itself as the subject area matured and merged into the international arena. International networks were formed, not least through subject societies and communities. Recruitment, too, became international, meaning that full professorships, as well as adjunct and visiting professorships, were advertised internationally. Researchers were invited to give talks or for shorter visiting spells. Joint applications were written even when funding calls were national. We argue that the shift from an environment where those researchers who were able to make a difference in the organisations they studied enjoyed high status to an environment where those who could say something very clever or smart about organisations were at the top of the pile happened naturally in this context.

Status now came from publication, citations and general recognition by other researchers and the community, not the firms and agencies they were studying. In fact, not even teaching kept its status. A new breed of researchers within business administration saw themselves not as teachers but purely as researchers; this created challenges, as many deans and department heads who work with planning can testify. There were exceptions to the rule, and we shall return to them in Section 3.3.4.

Bergkvist (2017) studied the status of so-called clinical research within management and strategy in Sweden and confirmed the aforementioned list of consequences. Bergkvist interviewed fifty prominent management and strategy professors in Sweden and concluded that clinical research was sparse and that 'empirical work' had taken its place. In addition, the main driving forces among researchers were to get published, cited and awarded with research grants. Less research time for seniors, lower ranking of practice-based research, and a poorly structured and managed 'third mission' (to collaborate with society, alongside research and teaching) were also identified as key factors behind the growing imbalance between rigour and relevance.

Global Firms

A final factor to bear in mind is that the character of firms across the world converged and the modern corporation was born, with fewer differences across countries and cultures. Partly as the result of the integration of the discipline, one can definitely say that the views of the firm, the object of analysis, converged, which probably also helped drive rigour over relevance. 'Now that we know what we're talking about we can divide the subject into categories (theoretical or empirical) and take it from there', so to speak. And the need to understand the local and the particular, and perhaps also the role of context, faded, in favour of general, universal theories that relied more on quantitative generalisation.

3.3 A New Era

The models and theories that have sprung out of the Swedish environment over the last three decades or so are less easy to distinguish from research output elsewhere. Swedish strategy research took on what we today might think of as 'normal' strategy research agendas, across Swedish institutions and also in relation to international ones. Here, the subjects, methods and approaches are less idiosyncratic and more in line with global strategy research virtues. Accordingly, we have structured the presentation here in relation to research areas rather than sites. The different research areas create a comprehensive menu of fairly typical strategy matters, globally speaking. One area concerns the macro-and-micro context of business (including internationalisation) and generally has a Porterian touch to it. Another area concerns boundary-spanning matters and inter-firm relations, including diversification, alliances and coopetition. A third area takes on the RBV, including exhaustive attempts to develop concepts such as knowledge, competence, capabilities and micro-foundations. Innovation and technology management, along with entrepreneurship, make up a fourth area. Finally, if the first four are often considered content-orientated, a fifth category is concerned more exclusively with process and strategy-as-practice.

In addition to these five subject areas we also discuss one prominent feature of strategy texts produced in Sweden in the 1990s: the ambition to explain to others (primarily Americans) the idiographic methods that are used in Sweden and what merits they might have. Several other Europeans have written about the same phenomenon (compare with Chakravarthy & Doz, 1992; Whittington, 1996; Johnson et al., 2007). Furthermore, we discuss a couple of examples of programmes that aimed at, and succeeded in, strengthening the relations between industry and academia to develop research agendas that benefit both sides, including the simultaneous pursuit of rigour and relevance.

3.3.1 International, National and Industry Competition

This is an area that to a certain degree is based on past efforts and success, such as the IIB at the SSE and the Uppsala group. However, it also takes the discipline further.

The IIB had good relations with two very important research nodes in strategy, namely Harvard Business School (HBS) and Stanford/Berkeley. Primarily through Örjan Sölvell, the collaboration with HBS, and particularly with Michael Porter, intensified during the 1980s and 1990s. Inspired by a guest visit to HBS at the beginning of the 1980s, Sölvell's research came to revolve around entry barriers and foreign penetration of national markets. Combining a traditional industrial organisation (IO) framework and theories of multinational enterprises, his doctoral dissertation (Sölvell, 1987) studied the foreign penetration of two industries in the field of electrical engineering. While many other Swedish strategy researchers at the time followed in the footsteps of Carlson and Mintzberg, and had a focus on strategy as a process, Sölvell turned to Porter and his IO research, and focused on linking strategy to the competitive environment. The important issue here was to explain which strategies give the firm competitive advantage. Sölvell and other Swedish researchers had a more international perspective than Porter, owing to Sweden being a much more internationalised and open economy. Thus, it was natural for Sölvell to combine Porter's frameworks with an international perspective that differentiated between national and international markets and penetration of these markets from abroad.

In Porter's (1990) *The Competitive Advantage of Nations*, the international competitiveness of firms is explained mainly by the structural characteristics of the domestic market. This book was the result of multinational empirical studies in ten countries in a number of different global industries. Sweden was one of the countries studied and the Swedish research team was led by Örjan Sölvell, assisted by Ivo Zander (brother of Udo Zander). The desire to describe more of the empirical material of the Swedish study led to the publication of a separate book, *Advantage Sweden* (Sölvell et al., 1991). While the Swedish studies to a large degree confirmed the Diamond framework, which, for example, suggests that Sweden has comparative advantages in industries that are dependent on raw materials such as iron ore and wood, as well as good supply of engineering knowledge, the rivalry factor caused some trouble for Porter (Porter, 1990, pp. 350–1). Porter viewed domestic rivalry, that is, several intensely competing firms in the same industry, as vital for development of successful international competitiveness. There are certainly examples of rivalry between leading firms in Swedish industries (e.g. Volvo and Scania, SCA and Stora). However, there are many more examples of industries that had only one leading firm with no domestic rival (e.g. Ericsson, Electrolux, Atlas Copco). Porter notes that the anti-trust laws in Sweden are not enforced for international industries because of the belief that it is necessary to operate on a large scale at home in order to meet global competition. This is a view that Porter disagrees with. Porter also notes that Swedish managers are taught to cooperate, not compete, and to solve industry problems by collective action. He admits that the absence of the rivalry factor in Sweden is partly compensated for by the strong incentives for growing Swedish firms to internationalise early and an unusually open economy that is thereby exposed to international competition at home. However, Porter believes that there is a price to pay for the lack of domestic rivalry, which is that only a narrow range of industries can become internationally competitive, such as industries where scale is important and there is limited scope for innovation activities. The Porter studies in international competitiveness led to the focus moving away from industry to clusters, that is, systems of interlinked industries, research organisations and authorities (Porter & Sölvell, 1998). Moreover, the competitiveness of firms was linked to the attractiveness of regions and nations.

In the period from the early 1980s to the end of the 1990s, the IIB at the SSE managed to substantially contribute to and influence the strategic management research field. But the IIB was closed down in 2005 and integrated into other research centres at the SSE. The SSE has continued to spawn excellent individual strategy researchers, such as Maria Bengtsson (a former doctoral student of Örjan Sölvell and now at Umeå University) on coopetition and Patric Regnér (e.g. 2003) on inductive and deductive strategy-making, but its position as an international and domestic focal point for high-quality strategy research is not as strong as it used to be.

The Uppsala model is prominent not least because it is still standing, so to speak, and being developed and discussed as a cornerstone in understanding the behaviour of firms as they expand abroad. Although alternative models have been developed, the Uppsala model is a must-cite when you do research on the challenges associated with the internationalisation process. However, as noted earlier, the non-strategic character of the Uppsala model (in the Uppsala researchers' own view) has received criticism not only from scholars of so-called born globals but also from closer to home, including their Uppsala colleagues and researchers on multinational strategies, such as Ulf Andersson, Mats Forsgren and Ulf Holm (e.g. Forsgren, 2002). These researchers view the MNC and its subsidiaries as embedded in external networks (Andersson & Forsgren, 1996), such as technical and business networks (Andersson et al., 2001, 2002). This view of the MNC, and particularly its subsidiaries, as embedded in different kinds of networks is partly influenced by another group of Uppsala researchers known as the IMP Group, which, since the mid-1970s, has contributed mainly to marketing research regarding the role of customer–supplier relationships, and other business relationships, in business-to-business (B2B) contexts (e.g. Håkansson & Snehota, 1995, 1998). In general, the IMP researchers are very critical towards a purely competitive view of customer–supplier relationships. They view these as collaborative relationships in which the customer and the supplier adapt to and develop each other over time.

3.3.2 Diversification, Alliances and Coopetition

Questions and challenges related to diversification, expansion and growth were long a popular field for Swedish strategy researchers. And the extended questions relating to growth management came to encompass matters related to partnering and managing ecosystems in the form of networks and alliances. The last thirty years of research have paralleled the perforation of value chains and the outsourcing of primarily productive functions overseas. The network constellations that surface as alternatives have been another key research topic and so have created a broad field of research on intra- and inter-organisational relations. Here we include not just diversification but also the management of alliances and coopetitors.

The strategy research carried out at Lund had strong historical links to the work of SIAR-ites and those close to Eric Rhenman. On his return from Harvard, Rhenman gradually phased out from his duties at the department. However, Lund had created the Institute of Economic Research, which came to focus in particular on strategy research questions. In the late 1980s, strategy positions were advertised and new agendas set. And honorary doctorates awarded: Mintzberg received his Dr.h.c. in 1989, and Jay Barney his in 1997, among others. Strategy became a formal subject division at Lund, although few other departments in the Swedish system followed suit. One of the PhD students hired was Rikard Larsson, who, we argue, is emblematic when it comes to illustrating the shift (see Section 3.2.4) that had taken place in the field in Sweden. Larsson gained his (second) PhD on mergers and acquisitions (M&A) and synergies in 1990 (he had already been awarded a PhD in the United States). Larsson was well-trained in statistical methods, compared to his predecessors, and he continued to experiment with methods throughout his active career. The typical monograph approach to dissertations that had dominated in Lund was not for Larsson, though. Among his articles, it is primarily the work on inter-organisational learning (Larsson et al., 1998) and synergy (Larsson & Finkelstein, 1999) that is well-cited, but he also wrote about M&A, management control, corporate alliances, internationalisation, strategic change and inter-organisational learning in different constellations with a respectable range of colleagues from all over the world.

The study of diversification, M&A and alliances continued strongly among colleagues in Lund, including Sven Collin and Lars Bengtsson. Bengtsson's (1993) thesis was a case study in the Rumeltian (Rumelt, 1974) tradition, focusing on diversification as a process of organic development and studying the control challenges that might occur as a consequence. Bengtsson continued to write on matters connected with diversification (e.g. Bengtsson, 2000), M&A, alliances (e.g. Larsson et al., 1998), organisational learning, knowledge and competence management, among other things.

Another Swedish scholar interested in diversification was Anders Pehrsson from Växjö. Växjö had otherwise profiled itself primarily within entrepreneurship. But Pehrsson was more interested in strategy and marketing. He gained his PhD from Linköping in 1986, and came to Växjö as a professor of strategy in 2000. Pehrsson's work is perhaps geared mainly towards internationalisation strategies and successful entry into new markets (Pehrsson, 2004, 2008, 2009, 2016), with, among other things, a focus on managerial and organisational challenges, such as seeking and reaping synergy potential. His most cited work, however, is his SMJ paper (Pehrsson, 2006), which is a large statistical survey into the concept of 'relatedness' in diversification research. Publishing in the SMJ is a rare achievement among Swedish strategy scholars, as is doing empirical research with a quantitative method. Pehrsson's approach is not without resemblance to Rikard Larsson's (Lund) approach: rigorous methodology, no stranger to statistical enquiry, and a clear and successful ambition to be part of the international strategy science arena and discourse. But it is still a unique approach in the Swedish context.

Umeå University was founded in 1965, and had research in business administration from the start. Like other departments of business administration, Umeå recruited from the more established departments and business schools in Sweden, and the Umeå School of Business and Economics was formed in 1989. One of the faculty members closest to strategy is Maria Bengtsson, who has published extensively on the subject of coopetition. Coopetition, in Bengtsson's approach, refers to simultaneous competition and cooperation between two or more actors in the same industry (i.e. competitors). Here, and unlike in other strands of research on coopetition, it is considered two-dimensional; coopetition is based on both competition and cooperation, simultaneously, whereas others typically see it as one-dimensional with competition and cooperation at the extremes (Bengtsson & Kock, 2014). Her most cited work, with Sören Kock from Hanken, Finland (Bengtsson & Kock, 2000), positions the approach on the same grounds as relationship theory, alliance theory and industry structure; coopetition makes sense, so to speak, in a context of inter-firm rivalry, competition and horizontal as well as vertical interactions. In that sense, the timing of Bengtsson's increased interest is perhaps emblematic for Swedish strategy research at the time: a combination of alliance and research on competition. Bengtsson has worked conceptually, primarily (with exceptions of course, e.g. Bengtsson & Sölvell, 2004), and pushed the field forward over the course of two decades.

In addition, Bengtsson's take on coopetition is not overly surprising, given the Swedish context, which we alluded to earlier. Yet another feature that Bengtsson has come to share with other Swedes, but was perhaps one of the first strategy researchers to acknowledge, is a growing fatigue against the dichotomy of the Porterian and the RBV approaches. Here, firm success and firm survival cannot be delimited exclusively to individual variables related to market position or resource endowments; rather, they must be related to the entire spectrum of competitive and cooperative efforts.

3.3.3 RBV, Knowledge and Cognition

A third area that Swedes have been interested in over the last thirty years or so can be thought of as the more micro-orientated matters surrounding strategic management, such as the resources, the knowledge assets and the cognitive ramifications of decision-making. These things have been popular objects of study at several institutions.

Udo Zander came out of the IIB community at the SSE and his dissertation project (Zander, 1991) concerned the diffusion and the replication of technological knowledge inside the multinational firm while trying to avoid knowledge leakage to competitors. Zander's dissertation project was to some extent connected to Hedlund's (Zander's supervisor) research on knowledge management, but was inspired more by US strategy and innovation management research, such as that undertaken by David Teece and Sidney Winter, and especially by Zander's collaboration with Bruce Kogut at Wharton. Zander's dissertation project combined some initial case studies in two Swedish major multinational companies in the paper-and-pulp and rock drilling industries, with a survey of company practices on knowledge diffusion and replication as well as imitation efforts from competitors. The study showed that Swedish MNCs rapidly diffuse and replicate innovations and introduce new products into foreign markets within a year on average, and notice imitation by competitors on average within eight years. One important result was that the time to imitation could be prolonged by employing a number of isolating mechanisms such as continuously developing the technology, using equipment and methods developed in-house and avoiding losing key employees.

The collaboration between Zander and Kogut started back in 1987 when Kogut was visiting the IIB. Together they started to develop the knowledge-based view of the multinational firm, criticising the then dominant transaction-cost theory perspective on multinational firms' strategic behaviour. They were inspired by early publications on RBV (e.g. Barney, 1986), technology transfer and rents (Teece, 1986), innovation diffusion (Rogers, 1983) and Winter's publication on knowledge and competence as strategic assets (Winter, 1987). In 1988 they submitted the first version of their *Organization Science* article (Kogut and Zander, 1992). The paper is one of the pioneering and most-referenced papers in the knowledge-based view of the firm research stream. One of the key concepts is 'combinative capabilities', that is, the innovative capability to re-combine current capabilities. In this way, they introduce a dynamic perspective on capabilities and resources, and at the same time imply that these combinative capabilities are internal and may be a source of competitive advantage. The concept of combinative capabilities foreshadows the more influential concept of dynamic capabilities introduced a couple of years later by Teece and Pisano (1994); they make reference to Kogut and Zander, with virtually the same meaning as combinative capabilities.

In Lund, Kristina Eneroth applied a resource-based approach to strategic competence development in high-tech firms (Eneroth, 1997), and with that became the first in a long line of Lundian PhD strategy students who embraced the RBV and carried out strategy process studies of the management of strategic resources. Jay Barney had been invited to Lund relatively soon after his 1991 classic and came regularly to give seminars throughout the 1990s. He was awarded an honorary doctorate in 1997, at a time when the RBV was not yet the dominant theory it would become. So the RBV was highly popular in Lund in the 1990s, much thanks to the efforts of Allan Malm (head of the strategy group) in connecting with such scholars, including also J.-C. Spender and later Nicolai Foss.

In the late 1990s and throughout the 2000s, Lundian strategy researchers started to work closely with industry, in projects called Learning Partnerships. The ambition was to obtain up-to-date data from firms that were keen to learn from academic research how they could improve in various areas. These partnerships typically revolved around practical problems that were interesting to study from a theoretical perspective, typically connected to the RBV. The Learning Partnership approach started in 1996 and continues to this day. More than twenty companies have been involved, in individual programmes, for long spells of time, including SCA, Trelleborg, Ericsson, E.ON, Vattenfall, Securitas, Assa Abloy, Axis Communications, Tetra Pak, the Swedish Institute for Standards and more. More than twenty PhD students and a multitude of publications (doctoral theses and papers) have so far come through the programme, all the while helping the firms with strategic decisions. The success factors include the ability to find and combine theoretically interesting questions with concrete challenges, and having practice-orientated PhD students who are keen on working close to real organisations. On the partner side, the main success factor is to actually have in place reflecting managers who understand the conditions of research and are themselves interested in theory and theoretical questions.

A lot of the empirical research done, by PhD students primarily, had a distinct RBV character. But as one of the main criticisms then (and still today) was that the RBV does not necessarily lend itself very well to statistical empirical enquiry, and because little had been done on the processes that firms go through as they manage their strategic resources to become VRIO, researchers should use the empirical proximity granted in the Learning Partnerships to gain inside knowledge and data on all sorts of intricate aspects surrounding the decisions and managerial and organisational processes underlying the formation of strategic resources. Kalling (1999) wrote about competitive advantage via what are known as Enterprise Resource Planning (ERP) systems, and Gibe (2007) studied how VRIO e-business capabilities are formed. Niklas Hallberg (2008) wrote about pricing capabilities, as did, later, Linn Andersson (2013), to mention but a few. All positioned their work in relation to the RBV and strategy process research, with qualitative approaches.

Another important area in the Swedish strategy tradition has been decision-making and the processes that decision-makers go through as they make sense of the world (e.g. Hedberg). One of the more prominent researchers in this field is Bo Hellgren from Linköping, who frequently worked with Melin. Hellgren has written extensively on the cognitive premises of strategy, including 'cognitive maps' (e.g. Hellgren & Löwstedt, 1997), strategists' 'ways-of-thinking' (Hellgren & Melin, 1993) and social theory and cognition (Hellgren & Löwstedt, 1998). Hellgren is a generalist and has also published extensively throughout his career in fields such as M&A, network organisations, strategy processes and collaborative strategies, to mention but a few.

Fredrik Tell came through the Linköping context but moved to Uppsala where he took over the chair that Carlson and Lars Engwall had occupied. There, he did research on various aspects of knowledge management in relation to strategy, among other things. Tell, too, is a generalist who has published in many different areas, including capabilities (Tell, 2000), open innovation (Bengtsson et al., 2015), innovation (Bergek et al., 2013), project management (Prencipe & Tell, 2001) and more. He is perhaps recognised mainly for his work on knowledge integration (e.g. Enberg et al., 2006; Lakemond et al., 2016; Tell et al., 2017). Here, Tell deals with the specialisation of knowledge, or, rather, how to manage several strands of specialised knowledge; this is a key concern for many knowledge management researchers since the field really started to take off within strategic management in the mid-1990s (e.g. Kogut & Zander, 1992; Nonaka, 1994; Grant, 1996; Spender, 1996). Tell's (2011) approach to knowledge integration suggests that it stems from task characteristics (e.g. degree of novelty, complexity), knowledge characteristics (e.g. tacitness, degree of differentiation) and relational characteristics (e.g. levels of inter-action) and can result in efficiency, effectiveness or innovation. In Tell's approach, the knowledge integration can help us understand several different matters, such as organisation, innovation and strategic change.

3.3.4 Tech, Innovation and Strategy at the Technical Institutes

Engineering researchers are typically no strangers to strategy, which is perhaps unsurprising: innovation often springs out of technological shifts; value-chain configuration requires analysis of logistics; and investment benefits from understanding technology. Different engineering institutions have contributed to the field of strategy, but we focus here on the work of a set of Chalmers researchers.

Chalmers University of Technology in Gothenburg is one of the more prominent education institutions in Sweden. Like many other technical institutions in Sweden, it is organised as a foundation; apart from research and education, it is also a centre for all kinds of entrepreneurial activities in the form of start-ups, incubators, joint ventures with industry and so on. Unsurprisingly, a lot of the collaboration activities are undertaken together with industry and firms in the Gothenburg and Southwest area of Sweden, typically represented by Volvo, SKF (the ball-bearings manufacturer), the shipping industry, the mechanical engineering industry and, in later years, in contexts of information technology (IT), nano technology and energy. Several engineers have made important contributions to management or strategy in the Swedish context. As an illustrative example: one of the more influential writers within strategy is Ove Granstrand (who studied at Stanford and gained his PhD from Chalmers) whose original field was operations management. Granstrand came to cover many areas, such as the organisation of research and development (R&D) and areas typically associated with strategy: growth, diversification, organisation culture, internationalisation, policy, financing, competence, innovation, intellectual capital and intellectual property (IP) law, and more (Granstrand, 2000).

One of the more interesting programmes in recent times, from a research organisation standpoint, was the Fenix Research Program (which has been described at length by Starkey & Madan, 2001), run under the auspices of the Institute for Management and Technology (IMIT). In the late 1990s, the Fenix programme was initiated as a collaboration between Chalmers and the SSE, and Volvo, Ericsson, Telia (a Swedish national telecoms operator) and AstraZeneca. The aim was to pinpoint and study research questions that were important for both academia and the industry partners. It was not explicitly stated as 'strategy', but the programme's overarching research question was the management of change in stable environments, studied from different angles. In the case of the work at Chalmers, this meant a particular focus on the challenges of the two Gothenburg-based partners, Volvo and AstraZeneca. The programme was led by senior researchers and professors, including Bengt Stymne (ex-SIAR, see Section 3.2.1). The bulk of the research was done by PhD students, appointed from within the partner companies to be industrial doctoral students. This arrangement, where top performers in firms are offered a part-time position as a PhD student in order to further themselves beyond, for example, MBA programmes, is quite common at technical institutions in Sweden. The theses that came out of Fenix typically dealt with issues related to organisational and strategic change.

The Fenix group were prolific when it came to arguing for their methodological approaches, with the anthologies *Collaborative Research in Organisations*

(Adler et al., 2004) and the *Handbook of Collaborative Management Research* (Shani et al., 2007) produced alongside papers by Jacob and colleagues (2000), Styhre and Sundgren (2005) and Adler and colleagues (2009). It should be noted that the Fenix programme was organised by the IMIT foundation, a large-scale home for industry–academy collaboration, primarily for the engineering sciences, which includes the Royal Institute of Technology, Chalmers, the Technical Institute at Lund, along with the SSE. The IMIT is a loosely coupled network of researchers who organise their collaboration with industry at the IMIT. The main objective, since its formation in 1979, has been to support technological, industrial and administrative renewal through research in collaborative form. Although the results of the research were intended primarily, if not exclusively, for the partner firms, and the general application outside the partner constellation was potentially limited, the approach definitely resembled that of the early SIAR group (as did the attempt at Lund with the Learning Partnerships). The majority of the PhD graduates that came through the programme went back to their employers full-time, but some stayed and pursued careers in academia, while others embarked on consulting. Fenix was dissolved in the late 2000s, but some of the faculty, including Flemming Norrgren and Tobias Fredberg, have continued to combine research with research-orientated consultancy in Truepoint, which combines research with practical, organisational challenges (see Eisenstat et al., 2008; Foote et al., 2011).

Researchers at the Royal Institute of Technology are also relatively active in innovation and other matters close to strategy, including Mats Magnusson (e.g. Björk & Magnusson, 2009), Mats Engwall (e.g. Tongur & Engwall, 2014) and Pontus Wadström (e.g. Wadström, 2020, 2022). Similarly, several researchers at the Technical Institute at Lund conduct research within strategy too, connected to business model innovation when companies face digitalisation and sustainability threats or opportunities, for instance Lars Bengtsson and the team around him (e.g. Wadin et al., 2017; Muhic & Bengtsson, 2021).

3.3.5 Strategy as Process and Practice

The popularity of the strategy-as-practice concept has perhaps not been as strong in Sweden as in other parts of Europe – and is perhaps stronger among organisation scholars. But it is certainly not surprising that a Swede took part in introducing the project. The inclusion of the manager and not just the organisation was a good match with the typical Swedish approach of working directly with decision-makers, who, in turn, were willing to share things that would have been treated as confidential in other places, or simply inaccessible. Melin was for a long time a staunch proponent of strategy process approaches. He worked with British process researchers such as Andrew Pettigrew, Gerry Johnson and Richard Whittington, all of whom were interested in what managers do when they manage strategies. The earlier strategy process research had been in decline during the 1990s, while research on strategic analysis and conceptual models of competitive advantage had become the norm (Johnson et al., 2003). Melin, Johnson and others put together a special issue of the *Journal of Management Studies* that was a call for studies at the micro level. The proposed research agenda (Johnson et al., 2003, p. 3) states: 'This paper argues for a shift in the strategy debate towards a micro perspective on strategy and strategizing. More specifically we are calling for an emphasis on the detailed processes and practices which constitute the day-to-day activities of organizational life and which relate to strategic outcomes.'

This stream of research soon became known as strategy-as-practice research, and Melin contributed to one of the first books in this stream (Johnson et al., 2007). Even though the strategy-as-practice papers by Melin do not mention Carlson's research as an inspiration for studies of managers' day-to-day activities, the link to Carlson's research is evident. We argue, in addition, that the line between Carlson's early behavioural project and the strategy-as-practice model connects a substantial amount of Swedish strategy research. However, apart from being one of the initiators, Melin has contributed a relatively sparse amount to the strategy-as-practice research.

The proponents of the strategy-as-practice perspective strongly disagree, but we certainly cannot refrain from connecting the strategy-as-practice approach and the process orientation of Swedish strategy research. Even if we accept that practice is a totally different thing, we would argue that it is not at all surprising that such a perspective emanates partly out of a Swedish context. The main contribution here, we argue, is to put the process perspective in more established theoretical quarters. Previously, the likes of the Chakravarthy and Doz (1992) article had been clear that strategy process, in an inductive sense, can be seen as inherently multidisciplinary. Challenges and solutions can be understood from different angles, for example economics, sociology, psychology. The findings and interests determine the choice of theory. Here, with the strategy-as-practice turn, the matter was positioned in relation to four schools of thought not unfamiliar to organisation scholars: the more micro-orientated approaches of the Carnegie tradition (e.g. cognitive matters, as discussed by Simon, March and Weick in various works) and the communities of the strategy-as-practice perspective (Lave & Wenger, 1991). They also added the more macro-orientated approaches of actor–network theory (Latour, 1987) and the under-standing of how individuals behave in networks of other people and artefacts, as well as neo-institutional theory (e.g. Scott, 1995). In the strategy-as-practice framework, strategic practice could be understood using one or more of these perspectives. While one can debate the practical benefits and whether this is strategy at all, the strategy-as-practice approach shed new light on what it means to be a decision-maker, a strategist, and did so with explicit distance from the typical American content approach. Today, however, little strategy research in Sweden sails under the strategy-as-practice flag.

3.3.6 'Methodenangst' ['Method Anxiety']

As should perhaps be evident by now, despite the many changes, one of the main features that very much remained intact during both the early and the later eras is the inclination to design empirical work as case studies. Statistical surveys have never taken off in Sweden, and, despite the fact that quantitative methods take up a substantial part of the PhD programme curricula, few strategy (or business admin) PhD students do that sort of research – which, of course, an American PhD student colleague, say, finds very peculiar. And in the early days, when research was local and not necessarily published in international journals, researchers did not lose any sleep over the way they went about their work. But as things turned international and the Swedes came to compete in an arena that is largely determined by the SMJ, ASQ and AoM communities, they realised that their method approaches were, repeatedly, deemed unscientific. Whereas one might have expected Swedes to use arguments about ontology and epistemology grounded in the philosophy of science (as they did early on, with the 'physics envy' concept), they instead took it upon themselves to describe and argue for the relative benefits of the case approach and how it can be combined with quantitative work. In the 1990s, particularly, much was written about the differences between the European and the American approaches (e.g. Bengtsson et al., 1997; Collin et al., 1996).

We have previously mentioned Rikard Larsson. He gained his first degrees in the American system, where quantitative methods dominate and case work and qualitative method were, at best, something to consider in teaching but of little use for an aspiring PhD student. Then, in coming back to the Swedish context, there was clearly room for concern. So Larsson wanted to combine the quantitative with the qualitative and published his ideas in the AoMJ (Larsson, 1993). The idea is quite simple, and Larsson used it himself extensively. The trade-off between aspect richness and number of observations is the main dilemma for a social science researcher. In an aspect-poor theory or hypothesis, you need multiple observations in order to accept or reject. However, in an aspect-rich context, that is, one with the typical complex frameworks and models used by social scientists – and Swedish strategy researchers – you need fewer cases to understand them in depth. Larsson used this method, which he called the 'case survey method', and 'borrowed' multi-case data from others to create his vast sets of qualitative data, so to speak. The approach never became a hit solution, but it highlighted a major issue for many of those in Sweden who wanted to become good, global, intra-paradigm strategy researchers. Other Swedish researchers, keen on making themselves understood by international (American) strategy researchers, continued to argue for the merits of what they often referred to as idiographic, as compared to nomothetic, research.

A couple of studies conducted by Swedes at the time underline the differences between North American and European research. Collin and colleagues (1996) studied the interchange of research across the Atlantic, based on the hypothesis that there are differences between American and European researchers when it comes to epistemology, ontology and methodology – which, as argued by the authors, is a sign of an undeveloped science compared to, say, medicine. Which, in turn, is true, or was, in the case of management studies in the early 1990s. Collin and colleagues (1996) studied the representation of Americans and Europeans in the four most prominent American journals and the four most prominent European journals.[8] The pattern was relatively clear. Europeans were not well-represented in the US journals, whereas Americans were well-represented in European journals. The authors suggested that this was owing either to American *reviewers* being less flexible and more bound to existing paradigms of objectivism (including positivism and determinism) or to European *authors* being too bound to their paradigm of subjectivism. The study did not say whether the low level of European representation was owing to there having been only a few European articles submitted to American journals or to the bulk of those submitted being rejected. On the other hand, either American *authors* were flexible enough to adhere to European paradigms or European *reviewers* were flexible enough to accept American objectivist approaches. Given that authors and reviewers jointly make up the research society, one might be tempted to suggest that European reviewers and American authors were more flexible to the other paradigm. Either way, the article clearly provided evidence for what many people already knew: that management studies is underdeveloped as a scientific field; that Americans lean toward objectivism and Europeans toward subjectivism; and that it is easier for the American approach(es) to find its way outside of its natural habitat.

---

[8] *Academy of Management Journal, Administrative Science Quarterly, Strategic Management Journal* and *Academy of Management Review* from America and *Human Relations, Organization Studies, Journal of Management Studies* and *British Management Journal* in Europe.

On the other hand, European acceptance of multiple paradigms is potentially an indication that the subject field is more diverse and developed in Europe.

Following on from what Collin and colleagues (1996) achieved, their contemporaries Bengtsson and colleagues (1997) took the question further, by arguing that the divide is unfortunate and that idiographic and nomothetic approaches could be combined, if not simultaneously at least over time. In this article, the authors discuss the premises under which European, idiographic research is or is not accepted for publication in American journals. They submitted a number of articles to prominent American journals that generally accept idiographic and qualitative research, in order to test feedback and to what extent reviewers understand idiographic research. The authors note that the nature of the idiographic research submitted is not very radical but adheres to principles suggested by Yin (1984) and Eisenhardt (1989), namely, principles that the staunchest positivist should be able to understand and relate to. Still the results are disappointing. According to the authors, the reviewers typically do not understand the logic of case research, although they claim to. They apply objectivist, positivist criteria to most instances, such as defining the research question, the selection and number of cases, the method(s) of data analysis, the use of existing literature and the theoretical contribution. Although it is clear that reviewers think that case-based idiographic research has a place in management research, such research is probably best suited to the early stages of projects. But the findings also unquestionably show that there is a clear transatlantic divide, and that idiographic researchers should reconsider their publication strategies: submit more surgically to those American journals that truly accept and understand idiographic research, or give up trying to share your research through American channels.

The attempts mentioned earlier, from the 1990s, are a sign of the times. Swedish researchers had a proper subject and a maturing global strategy community, they had realised and mastered paper writing and publishing in international journals, and they wanted to take part. But the traditional, case-based, idiographic approach, inherited through decades of research governed by norms stipulating that it is good to be close to data and the real world, the decision-makers, that it is good to be relevant, and of course that we can learn from the particular, the individual case: that approach was difficult to carry into the global community. A period of schizophrenia emerged as Swedish strategy researchers tried to adhere to positivist, nomothetic approaches and at the same time argue for their approach, usually in vain, as there is little evidence that anything has changed. Today, this schizophrenia is not as strong; most Swedish researchers gave up trying to do research in a positivist fashion and, consequently, publish in less significant outlets, or concentrate on writing high-quality conceptual pieces. As is noted by Schriber (2016), part of the reason the overlap between Swedes and others is now larger is that the objects of study typical to Swedish and Nordic researchers have become more popular in the global community. Schriber mentions knowledge, capabilities and resources, that is, organisation-internal factors.

In sum, while many methodological changes have taken place, approaches including case work, typically with a process orientation, or purely conceptual research, still dominate the field in Sweden. Having access to data from companies and managers and not being dependent only on public databases is still considered to be a good thing. Other things have changed more drastically, however, such as the propensity to focus on rigour rather than relevance. Although there are exceptions, in general much strategy research from Sweden gave up on applying and 'helping out' as there is no merit associated with it in the international arena – or in Sweden. The engineering ethos is in decline, and although a lot of interesting, scientifically well-grounded research is produced, the relevance component is weak even if there are promising exceptions, which we have touched upon already. Furthermore, industry representatives are typically prepared to open up in conversations with researchers, so there is undoubtedly fertile ground for the clinically orientated scholar.

4 Conclusions

In this volume we have described the development of Swedish strategy research and tried to identify why and how the field gradually moved from relevance to rigour as its main virtue. Theory suggests that it is a question of knowledge differences and institutional forces, and we can certainly say we see these factors at play in the Swedish case: the entry of consulting firms, the integration of a global scientific discipline along with isomorphism on behalf of global firms, and policy reforms for the higher education sector carry both knowledge differences and institutional forces. In our case we would, however, suggest that we add, as a fundamental factor, the possibility for cultural change, meaning the abandonment, temporary or not, of century-long ideals for scholarship and research in favour of, to put it bluntly, different ideals. The knowledge transfer and relational factors should be seen as the result of deeper movements and mechanisms in the world of academia and the society and politics that shape it. Next, we touch on both layers of explanations, and discuss the forces that might help balance the current rigour–relevance position.

4.1 Factors of Change

4.1.1 Knowledge Differences

Starkey and Madan's (2001) suggestion that the rigour–relevance gap might depend on the different nature of knowledge is supported in this case: although

Mode 2 was dominant in the early stages, it gradually became Mode 1 in Sweden. Van de Ven and Johnson's (2006) idea that it is a knowledge transfer problem may also hold true in the Swedish case. Both these theories are supported or illustrated here, but at the same time we can clearly see that there was a time when they were not an issue; in the early days, there was a significant overlap across academia and practice, at least enough for a conversation to take place across the two sectors. The evidence-based movement's (Rousseau, 2006, 2007) take that we need to work with models based on single case studies that, evidently, can be applied across cases happened in Sweden from the start. That was the whole idea of the SIAR 'territory' concept and one of the reasons why it came to focus on industry logics, so there is not much new there. The evidence-based argument can be partly resolved by, for example, applying a case methodology logic, particularly that known as analytical generalisation (Yin, 1984).

This was also the fundamental question for SIAR researchers (Lind & Rhenman, 1989), who constantly struggled with how observations of the particular could be made useful to the universal. The real answer here is probably *specialisation*. As discussed earlier, two knowledge-related forces offer an answer, and both of them depend on endogenous and exogenous factors: the emergence of a *consultancy market* (driven by soaring demand and an increasingly uncompetitive academic sector) and the emergence and forming of a *global society of strategy researchers* (in our case, driven more or less entirely by the formation of the SMS, which was determined to promote 'hard science'). Both sides, the academic and the consulting, were subject to severe competition; in order to stay competitive, specialisation was needed, and it happened implicitly and explicitly. It also became more difficult to master both sides of the operation. As a consequence, the knowledge overlap diminished and made it less likely that collaboration would be fruitful to both sides. We would argue, however, that the Swedish case offers recent examples where there is a will on both sides to collaborate because they share, at least temporarily, language and can merge their respective ambitions to improve and to learn. Swedish executives are typically keen to share and to take time for interviews with academics. The fact that the connection between industry and academia (such as in the case of Fenix and the Learning Partnerships in Lund) is still there is good news in our book, but at the same time it is testament to an environment where there is a significant lack of will to reach out among enough Swedish scholars. Perhaps the many years of keeping apart have not only deepened the cognitive separation but also developed a culture, a norm, that supports the idea that collaboration is not important, or at least weakened the norm that said it is important. Going back to the features that characterised Swedish strategy research initially, we indicated that many of them prevail but that, first and foremost, the will to help improve – the engineering ethos – has become less of a priority. In this, the knowledge differences should be supplemented by cultural differences. Sweden has bought into a norm system that is not in line with the existing culture.

4.1.2 Relations and Institutions

In their seminal study of articles published between 1980 and 2005, Agarwal and Hoetker (2007) found that the field of management studies could be said to have grown up. The proportion of references to economics and sociology had been reduced and the integrated management field had become a valid discipline in its own right. One problem with this, according to the authors, was that this came with incessant focus on rigour, which in turn had shifted the focus far away from relevance, to the extent that the frameworks 'do not inform those who manage firms and lead people' (Agarwal and Hoetker, 2007, p. 1319). According to Agarwal and Hoetker (2007), this can all be related to what Whitley (1984) refers to as subject integration. In this context, we need to work with policymaking. And that is another field that is often under-discussed in gap theory and in empirical studies. In our case, the Swedish *university reform* in 1993 certainly pushed things in the direction of rigour, as we discussed in Section 3.2.4. The withholding of research grants, competitive calls, international collaboration, a focus on PhD students, the separation of teaching and researching, along with other measures, all helped change matters.

Gap theory has suggested a range of relational and institutional forces, including 'integrative scholarship' (Bartunek, 2007; Bartunek & Rynes, 2010), as well as a range of differences between the business world and the academic world, such as time perspectives and communication forms. Our study finds no reason to doubt these suggestions; they surface in our material as well. And we can only concur. Of course it would be good if we could bridge institutional differences and strengthen relations; we have seen recent examples in the Swedish case of how one can go about this. Swedish industry and academia can collaborate as long as there is some form of perceived relevance involved. And that is one institutional force to build on: Swedish firms have not given up entirely on academic collaboration, and there are still strategy researchers who are keen on relevance and reaching out. Finding trust in these relations is a way forward if one has any interest in relevance.

Furthermore, as indicated in our findings, the fact that *firms become more similar*, thereby decreasing the uncertainty about the object of study (Whitley, 1984), is another institutional force in its own right, making the subject field more mature but at the same time more subjected to 'theoretical parochialism'.

However, one might be tempted to claim that this isomorphism, too, is happening under the auspices of American industry and American business schools, and so further claim that the establishment of the field is ultimately an affair designed by the way the United States approached management education in the 1950s and since.

4.1.3 'Scientification'

We do think that Khurana's (2007) take on the field of management and the role of the foundation reports partly explains the Swedish case too, even if it took at least a decade longer to happen in Sweden. It serves as a fundamental explanation for both the knowledge issues and the matters connected to relations and institutions. The split into disciplines and the move away from a general management focus, and the conditioned grant system, also happened in Sweden. Some things did not happen to the same extent, such as quantification, but, as this was spread not via the political or government systems but via the subject connections, it came to Sweden and eventually meant that rigour was the main virtue; relevance was crowded out and taken care of by consultants (who gradually also took over any relevance-orientated research). One other interesting observation is the kinship during the early era between HBS and various Swedish institutions: Eric Rhenman was a professor at HBS, and Richard Normann was a visiting professor there in the 1980s, which explains, we argue, much of SIAR's approach. Michael Porter visited Sweden and there were numerous connections between the faculties of HBS and the SSE. As indicated in Khurana's (2007) study, HBS was *one* institution, perhaps the only one, that really managed to maintain a case-based, generalist approach to management throughout the transformation that came as a result of, among other things, the implementation of the advice offered by the foundation reports.

In addition, we believe that much of what happened can also be explained by Whitley's (1984) approach. Much of the history of strategy research bears strong resemblance to his chronological framework, in which subjects are integrated and the objects of study become less uncertain. It might be that the forming of a consultancy market is partly the result of poorer performance among academics when it comes to relevance, which in part might be owing to their focusing on rigour, a consequence of the integration of the subject field. And the formation of the global community of strategy researchers is without question an example of subject integration. In that sense, we should not be surprised about what happened in the Swedish case. Still, what matters is that the path chosen was the American. And why this was the case is a key question, and a difficult one. We guess that the answer might lie in the cultural dominance in the post–World War II era, the power of American companies, the increasing American focus on domination in all areas including science, the arts, culture and more. It was in this era and in this zeitgeist that the foundation reports were published, and the American business schools, not the European ones, took the lead and developed curricula and set standards for research. Perhaps the whole thing boils down to the situation post–World War II: the Americans and the Russians were victorious and the Cold War was initiated, including the science race, which spilled over into management education; continental Europe was in ruins, Marshall Plan much appreciated but a 'peace' on American terms. It is not surprising that European countries came to mimic American approaches to science and management studies and tried to adjust, sometimes without actually sharing the ontological and epistemological standpoints. The coming about of strategy happened to coincide with the aftermath of World War II and the commencement of the Cold War, which explains why it turned out the way it did. At the same time, the German ideals and logics that had been more powerful before the wars had lost their allure, for many reasons.

4.1.4 A Fundamental Explanation

Although it is tempting to draw a causal line between World War II, the foundation reports and the transformation into hard science and rigour and challenges in relation knowledge, relations and institutions, we must be cautious. The four key factors (that actually helped drive rigour at the expense of relevance) in the case of Swedish strategy can all be identified as the theoretically presumed issues related to knowledge, relations and institutional forces. In turn, Khurana's (2007) argument may well be used, although it is skating on thin ice to say that these presumed factors can be connected to the foundation reports and the other forces at play at around the same time.

We suggest that this chain of events actually has a bearing on the current status of the rigour–relevance gap, but it might not matter; fundamental ideals of how to conduct social science research clashed and were challenged, and centuries-old ideals were partly replaced. The factors we have listed probably all carry explanatory capacity, but the conclusion is that something more fundamental than knowledge, relations and institutions changed too; this is perhaps best referred to as research culture. In this case, it is a centuries-long culture that in some ways was partly (re)shaped by the more fundamental forces discussed in this Element. The important message, however, is that although Swedish strategy research lost, or rather played down, something that had proved important for relevance and for the position of strategy (and social science) research in society, many of these forces are still in place; they have been used recently and they can be used again. There is fertile ground among industry representatives, and if the academic side (or enough of its members) could alter its views on empirical work, we would experience a re-balance of rigour and relevance.

4.2 Lessons Learned

We suggest that much of the rigour–relevance debate could benefit from thinking slightly more deeply than about mere knowledge transfer factors, relations or even direct institutional forces. In the slow-moving academic world, one probably also benefits by looking at longer periods. There is no question that knowledge differences, relations and institutions (such as university policies) play a part, but a thorough understanding must go beyond that by looking into deeper ideals and how they can resist, or not, new influences. What we have seen shares many attributes with earlier events and passages in history, such as the eighteenth-century divide between mercantilists (e.g. Dutch and British) and 'reform mer-cantilists' (e.g. cameralists in Germany and Scandinavia) in which one of the big questions was the extent to which government should intervene in commerce. Even among cameralists there were conflicts between practitioners and academics and also between academics who favoured the new subject's position in curricula and those who did not. Likewise, the *Methodenstreit* of the late nineteenth and early twentieth centuries also holds features that are similar to the tensions reported in this case: the German historiographic approach versus the Austrian 'exact' science.

The Swedish case illustrates many aspects of the gap challenge: it shows how rigour and relevance can be combined, but also how this balance can vanish. The case also brought up a number of models that have stood the test of time and still have some international meaning: the stakeholder model (Rhenman & Stymne, 1965), models of the internationalisation process (Johanson & Vahlne, 1977), the business idea (Rhenman, 1969a), nowadays referred to as the business model, combinative capabilities (now dynamic capabilities) (Kogut & Zander, 1992) and more, typically based on case studies of Swedish companies. On the occasions that Swedes have been successful academically, it is when they have applied historical virtues such as empirical proximity, with orientations towards the idiographic and processes with the explicit aim of helping decision-makers. The focus on internationalisation and the idiographic research approach are still being used, as is, to a certain extent, the systemic nature of Swedish models, whereas the desire to apply and help improve has become less prominent. The relation between industry and academia is, however, still relatively vital. Recent examples of collaboration indicate this. There are still industry leaders willing to reach out and understand the role of rigour and relevance. We believe that the current Swedish situation is a product not so much of deep cultural changes but of adhering to international routines and standards. Some of the Swedish virtues have remained intact. In many ways, the rigour–relevance gap is an American problem that others, such as Sweden, bought into as they joined the international research community, because it was there and everybody else was joining it. Like a Pax Americana. And a great deal of good research came out of it, although it was perhaps more rigorous than relevant.

So, what can one do in the Swedish context and elsewhere? Well, one first reaction may well be that this is in order and the way things should be; that what we have seen in the Swedish case is a straightforward example of Whitley's (1984) take on how subjects mature through integration and through the increasing understanding of the object of study; that this is natural and that the divide between research and practice is insurmountable (e.g. Daft & Lewin, 2008; Kieser & Leiner, 2009). The problem with this approach, we fear, is that research grants might be at risk as politicians and other financiers of research simply lose faith and cut budgets – for both research and education. Neither public nor private financiers are likely to support something as mundane and insignificant as strategy and business administration (compared to, say, medicine) if there are no signs of benefits to industry or society.

However, for those who are keen on re-balancing rigour and relevance, this case has shown how it can be done. The case methodology works in many instances, and unquestionably so in early-stage research. Process-based research has merits when it comes to understanding complex processes laid out over time. Add to that the close relations to industry and we have fertile ground for in-depth studies of key business transformation patterns. A lot can be done in the policy arena, at government level, but that is a cumbersome process. Spending, the teaching/research proportions, salary levels, tenure, PhD studies, could all be modified to make our work more relevant. But, university policy aside, there is a lot of freedom to decide for ourselves, as professors, how we define subjects and recruit, as well as how we collaborate with outside organisations. Working more closely with engineering institutes, together with industry, would also help bring relevance back – and bring out the engineering ethos that is probably still there in sufficient numbers of strategy researchers. As we have seen, this was a success factor in the past. So it is really down to the field itself, if only the research leaders are interested. Perhaps the prospect of losing grants can act as an incentive, if the direct desire to work closely with firms and agencies is not strong enough.

The culture of relevance, for lack of a better word, is still there, on both sides, albeit impaired. But Swedes and other Europeans have been doing research and helped in the administration and management of industry and public agency in collaborative form for more than 300 years; it is probably time to revisit some of those principles and ways of operating, in the event that we want to increase the relevance and the usefulness of our labour.

We realise that the discussion of rigour and relevance ultimately means that we must ask ourselves why we should have business schools at all, or at least what kind of roles and functions business schools should have. One might lean towards the pure focus on scientific rigour; one might think we should go back to the days of night schools and a highly practical approach. This is a topic for another text, but in our humble view we see three functions for the future business school: the 'science' function; the 'clinical' function; and, which we haven't discussed much in this text, a 'political' or 'critical' function where the negative externalities of business schools are being researched. This probably means not that every business school should have an equal portion of each but that schools will specialise. We assume that the 'clinical' function will regain its prominence.

References

Adler, N., Elmquist, M., & Norrgren, F. (2009). The challenge of managing boundary-spanning research activities: experiences from the Swedish context. *Research Policy, 38*(7), 1136–49.

Adler, N., Shani, R., & Styhre, A. (eds.) (2004). *Collaborative Research in Organisations: Foundations for Learning, Change and Theoretical Development.* Thousand Oaks, CA: Sage.

Agarwal, R., & Hoetker, G. (2007) A Faustian bargain? The growth of management and the relationship with related disciplines. *Academy of Management Journal, 50*(6), 1304–22.

Ahlmann, H., & Rhenman, E. (1964). *Rationaliseringsarbete. Organisation och Planering. En systematik och nyare teori tillämpad på en specialistavdelnings organisationsproblem [Rationalisation Work – Organisation and Planning: A Systematics and Recent Theory Applied to a Specialist Department's Organizaitonal Problem].* Stockholm: Norstedts.

Andersson, L. (2013). *Pricing capability development and its antecedents.* Doctoral thesis. Lund University.

Andersson, U., & Forsgren, M. (1996). Subsidiary embeddedness and control in the multinational corporation. *International Business Review, 5*(5), 487–508.

Andersson, U., Forsgren, M., & Holm, U. (2001). Subsidiary embeddedness and competence development in MNCs: a multi-level analysis. *Organization Studies, 22*(6), 1013–34.

Andersson, U., Forsgren, M., & Holm, U. (2002). The strategic impact of external networks: subsidiary performance and competence development in the multinational corporation. *Strategic Management Journal, 23*(11), 979–96.

Andrésen, A.-M., Kalling, T., & Wikström, K. (2012). *The Rise and Fall of the Scandinavian Institutes for Administrative Research (SIAR): Lessons Learned from a Nordic Management Consulting Pioneer.* Lund: Lund Business Press.

Andrews, K., Learned, E., Christensen, R., & Guth, W. (1965). *Business Policy: Texts and Cases.* Homewood, IL: Irwin.

Ansoff, I. (1965). *Corporate Strategy: An Analytical Approach to Business Policy for Growth and Expansion.* New York: McGraw-Hill.

Ashby, W. R. (1956). The effect of experience on a determinate dynamic system. *Behavioral Science, 1*(1), 35–42.

Augier, M., & March, J. G. (2007). The pursuit of relevance in management education. *California Management Review, 49*(3), 128–46.

Baldridge, D. C., Floyd, S. W., & Markóczy, L. (2004). Are managers from Mars and academicians from Venus? Toward an understanding of academic quality and practical relevance. *Strategic Management Journal, 25*(11), 1063–74.

Barnard, C. (1938). *The Functions of the Executive.* Cambridge, MA: Harvard University Press.

Barney, J. B. (1986). Organizational culture: can it be a source of sustained competitive advantage? *Academy of Management Review, 11*(3), 656–65.

Barney, J. B. (1991). Firm resources and sustained competitive advantage. *Journal of Management, 17*(1), 99–120.

Bartunek, J. M. (2007). Academic-practitioner collaboration need not require joint or relevant research: toward a relational scholarship of integration. *Academy of Management Journal, 50*(6), 1323–33.

Bartunek, J. M., & Rynes, S. L. (2010). The construction of 'implications for practice': what's in them and what might they offer? *Academy of Management Learning and Education, 9*(1), 100–17.

Bartunek, J. M., & Rynes, S. L. (2014). Academics and practitioners are alike and unlike: the paradoxes of academic-practitioner relationships. *Journal of Management, 40*(5), 1181–201.

Bengtsson, L. (1993). *Intern diversifiering som strategisk process [Internal diversification as a strategic process].* Doctoral thesis. Lund University.

Bengtsson, L. (2000). Corporate strategy in a small open economy: reducing product diversification while increasing international diversification. *European Management Journal, 18*(4), 444–53.

Bengtsson, L. (2004). Explaining born globals: an organisational learning perspective on the internationalisation process. *International Journal of Globalisation and Small Business, 1*(1), 28–41.

Bengtsson, L., Elg, U., & Lind, J.-I. (1997). Bridging the transatlantic publishing gap: how North American reviewers evaluate European idiographic research. *Scandinavian Journal of Management, 13*(4), 473–92.

Bengtsson, M., & Kock, S. (2000). 'Coopetition' in business networks: to cooperate and compete simultaneously. *Industrial Marketing Management, 29*(5), 411–26.

Bengtsson, M., & Kock, S. (2014). Coopetition: quo vadis? Past accomplishments and future challenges. *Industrial Marketing Management, 43*(2), 180–8.

Bengtsson, L., Lakemond, N., Lazarotti, V., et al. (2015). Open to a select few? Matching partners and knowledge content for open innovation performance. *Creativity and Innovation Management, 24*(1), 72–86.

Bengtsson, M., & Sölvell, Ö. (2004). Climate of competition, clusters and innovative performance. *Scandinavian Journal of Management, 20*(3), 225–44.

Bennis, W. G., & O'Toole, J. (2005). How business schools have lost their way. *Harvard Business Review, 83*(5), 96–104.

Berch, A. (1749). *Tal om den proportion, som de studerande ärfordra til de ledige beställningar i riket (Speech about the skill sets necessary for available positions in government]*. Speech given to students in Uppsala. Stockholm: Printed by L. Salvius (in Swedish).

Bergek, A., Berggren, C., Magnusson, M., & Hobday, M. (2013). Technological discontinuities and the challenger for incumbent firms: destruction, disruption or creative accumulation? *Research Policy, 42*, 1210–24.

Bergkvist, T. (2017). *På jakt bland forskare och managementkonsulter [Looking for Researchers and Management Consultants]*. Rapport VR 2017:04. Stockholm: Vinnova (Verket för Innovationssystem [Swedish Governmental Agency for Innovation Systems]).

Birkinshaw, J., Lecuona, R., & Barwise, P. (2016). The relevance gap in business school research: which academic papers are cited in managerial bridge journals? *Academy of Management Learning & Education, 15*(4), 686–702.

Björk, J., & Magnusson, M. (2009). Where do good innovation ideas come from? Exploring the influence of network connectivity on innovation idea quality. *Journal of Product Innovation Management, 26*(6), 662–70.

Bower, J. L. (1970). Planning within the firm. *American Economic Review, 60*(2), 186–94.

Bruzelius, L., & Skärvad, P.-H. (1974). *Integrerad administrationslära [Integrated Administration Theory]*. Malmö: Liber.

Burgelman, R. A. (1983). Corporate entrepreneurship and strategic management: Insights from a process study. *Management Science, 29*(12), 1349–64.

Burgelman, R. A. (1988). Strategy making as a social learning process: The case of internal corporate venturing. *Interfaces, 18*(3), 74–85.

Burns, T., & Stalker, G. M. (1961). *The Management of Innovation*. London: Tavistock.

Carlson, S. (1951). *Executive Behavior*. Stockholm: Strömbergs.

Carlson, S. (1964). *Development Economics and Administration*. Stockholm: Svenska Bokförlaget.

Carlson, S. (1966). *International Business Research*. Uppsala: Uppsala University Press.

Carlson, S. (1975). *How Foreign Is Foreign Trade? A Problem in International Business Research*. Uppsala: Uppsala University Press.

Carlsson, R. H. (ed.) (2000). *SIAR – Strategier för att tjäna pengar [SIAR – Strategies to Make Money]*. Stockholm: Ekerlids Förlag.

Carlsson, R. H. (2013). *Tidig med allt. Alltid före sin tid. Biografi över Eric Rhenman [Early With Everything. Always Ahead of His Time. Biography of Eric Rhenman]*. Stockholm: Ekerlids Förlag.

Chakravarthy, B. S., & Doz, Y. (1992). Strategy process research: focusing on corporate self-renewal. *Strategic Management Journal, 13*(S1), 5–14.

Chandler, A. D. (1962). *Strategy and Structure: Chapters in the History of the Industrial Empire*. Cambridge, MA: MIT Press.

Chandler, A. D. (1977). *The Visible Hand: The Managerial Revolution in American Business*. Cambridge, MA: Belknap Press.

Chandler, A. D. (1990). *Scale and Scope: The Dynamics of Industrial Capitalism*. Cambridge MA: Harvard University Press.

Childs, M. W. (1936). *Sweden: The Middle Way*. New Haven, CT: Yale University Press.

Collin, S. O., Johansson, U., Svensson, K., & Ulvenblad, P. O. (1996). Market segmentation in scientific publications: research patterns in American vs European management journals. *British Journal of Management, 7*(2), 141–54.

Cyert, R. M., & March, J. G. (1963). *A Behavioral Theory of the Firm*. Englewood Cliffs, NJ: Prentice Hall.

Daft, R. L., & Lewin, A. Y. (2008). Perspective – rigor and relevance in organization studies: idea migration and academic journal evolution. *Organization Science, 19*(1), 177–83.

Dahlqvist, K., Eriksson, L., & Fritzell, A. (2019). *Mål- och resultatstyrning i staten – vad vi sett och insett: med fokus på universitets- och högskolepolitik 1988–1995 inom utbildningsdepartementet [Objectives- and Output-Based Control in the State – What We Have Seen and Realised: With a Focus on University and Higher Education Policy 1988–1995 within the Minstry of Education]*. Stockholm: Kungliga Musikhögskolan.

Eisenhardt, K. M. (1989). Building theories from case study research. *Academy of Management Review, 14*(4), 532–50.

Eisenstat, R. A., Beer, M., Foote, N., Fredberg, T., & Norrgren, F. (2008). The uncompromising leader. *Harvard Business Review, 86*(7–8), 50–7.

Enberg, C., Lindkvist, L., & Tell, F. (2006). Exploring the dynamics of knowledge integration: acting and interacting in project teams. *Management Learning, 37*(2), 143–65.

Eneroth, K. (1997). *Strategi och kompetensdynamik: en studie i Axis Communications [Strategy and competence dynamics: a study in Axis Communications]*. PhD thesis. Lund University.

Engwall, L. (1986). Mercury meets Minerva. *Scandinavian Journal of Management Studies*, *3*(2), 121–38.

Engwall, L. (2020). *Fenomenet Företagsekonomi [The Phenomenon of Business Administration]*. Lund: Studentlitteratur.

Engwall, L., Kipping, M., & Üsdiken, B. (2010). Public science systems, higher education and the trajectory of academic disciplines: business studies in the United States and Europe. In R. Whitley, J. Glaser & L. Engwall (eds.), *Reconfiguring Knowledge Production: Changing Authority Relationships in the Sciences and the Consequences for Intellectual Innovation*, 325–53. Oxford: Oxford University Press.

Foote, N., Eisenstat, R., & Fredberg, T. (2011). The higher ambition leader. *Harvard Business Review*, *89*(9), 94–105.

Forsgren, M. (2002). The concept of learning in the Uppsala internationalization process model: a critical review. *International Business Review*, *11*(3), 257–77.

Forsgren, M. (2016). A note on the revisited Uppsala internationalization process model: the implications of business networks and entrepreneurship. *Journal of International Business Studies*, *47*(9), 1135–44.

Forsgren, M. (2017). *Theories of the Multinational Firm: A Multidimensional Creature in the Global Economy*. Cheltenham: Edward Elgar.

Freeman, R. E. (1984). *Stakeholder Management: Framework and Philosophy*. Mansfield, MA: Pitman.

Freeman, R. E. (2010). *Strategic Management: A Stakeholder Approach*. Cambridge: Cambridge University Press.

Friedman, M. (1970). A Friedman doctrine: the social responsibility of business is to increase its profits. *New York Times Magazine*, *13*(1970), 32–3.

Galbraith, J. (1973). *Designing Complex Organizations*. Reading, MA: Addison-Wesley.

Gibbons, M., Limoges, L., Nowotny, H., Schwartman, S., Scott, P., & Trow, M. (1994). *The New Production of Knowledge: The Dynamics of Science and Research in Contemporary Societies*. London: Sage.

Gibe, J. (2007). *The microstructure of collaborative e-business capability*. PhD thesis. Lund University.

Gioia, D. (2022). On the road to hell: why academia is viewed as irrelevant to practicing managers. *Academy of Management Discoveries*, *8*(2), 174–9.

Gordon, R. A., & Howell, J. E. (1959). *Higher Education for Business*. New York: Columbia University Press.

Granstrand, O. (2000). The shift towards intellectual capitalism: the role of infocom technologies. *Research Policy*, *29*(9), 1061–80.

Grant, R. M. (1996). Toward a knowledge-based theory of the firm. *Strategic Management Journal*, *17*(S2), 109–22.

Grimmer-Solem, E. (2003). *The Rise of Historical Economics and Social Reform in Germany, 1864–1894*. Oxford: Oxford University Press.

Håkansson, H., & Snehota, I. (1995). *Developing Relationships in Business Networks*. London: Routledge.

Håkansson, H., & Snehota, I. (1998). The burden of relationships or who's next. In P. Naude & P. W. Turnbull (eds.), *Network Dynamics in International Marketing*, 16–25. Oxford: Pergamon.

Hallberg, N. (2008). *Pricing capability and its strategic dimensions*. PhD thesis. School of Economics and Management, Lund University.

Hambrick, D. C. (1994). What if the academy actually mattered? *Academy of Management Review*, *19*(1), 11–16.

Hedberg, B. (1971). *On man-computer interaction in organizational decision-making: a behavioral approach*. PhD thesis. Gothenburg University.

Hedberg, B. (ed.) (1994). *Imaginära organisationer [Imaginary Organisations]*. Malmö: Liber-Hermod.

Hedberg, B., Edström, A., Müller, W., & Wilpert, B. (1975). *The Impact of Computer Technology on Organizational Power Structures*. Berlin: Walter de Gruyter.

Hedberg, B., & Ericson, A. (1979). *Insiktströghet och manövertröghet i organisationers omorientering [Insight Inertia and Manoevre Inertia in Organisations' Reorientation]*. Research Report. Gothenburg University.

Hedberg, B., & Jönsson, S. (1977). Strategy formulation as a discontinuous process. *International Studies of Management and Organization*, *7*(2), 88–109.

Hedberg, B., & Jönsson, S. (1978). Designing semi-confusing information systems for organizations in changing environments. In C. Emmanuel, D. Otley & K. Merchant (eds.), *Readings in Accounting for Management Control*, 149–73. Boston, MA: Springer.

Hedberg, B., & Jönsson, S. (1989). Between myth and action. *Scandinavian Journal of Management*, *5*(3), 177–85.

Hedberg, B. L., Nystrom, P. C., & Starbuck, W. H. (1976). Camping on seesaws: prescriptions for a self-designing organization. *Administrative Science Quarterly*, *21*(1), 41–65.

Hedberg, B., Sjöberg, S., & Targama, A. (1972). *Styrsystem och företagsdemokrati [Management Systems and Corporate Democracy]*. Gothenburg: Centraltryck.

Hedberg, B., & Sjöstrand, S. E. (1979). *Från företagskriser till industripolitik [From Corporate Crises to Industrial Politics]*. Malmö: Liber.

Hedlund, G. (1976). *Det multinationella företaget, nationalstaten och fackföreningarna: en diskussion av utgångspunkter och metoder [The Multinational Corporation, the State and the Trade Unions: A Discussion of Approaches and Methods]*. Stockholm: Ekonomiska Forskningsinstitutet vid Handelshögskolan (EFI) [Economic Research Institutes at the School of Economics].

Hedlund, G. (1986). The hypermodern MNC – a heterarchy? *Human Resource Management*, 25(1), 9–35.

Hedlund, G. (1994). A model of knowledge management and the N-form corporation. *Strategic Management Journal*, 15(S2), 73–90.

Hedlund, G., & Nonaka, I. (1993). Models of knowledge management in the West and Japan. In P. Lorange, B. Chakravarthy, J. Ross & A. Van de Ven (eds.), Implementing Strategic Processes: Change, Learning, and Cooperation, 117–44. London: Macmillan.

Hellgren, B., & Löwstedt, J. (1997). *Tankens företag: kognitiva kartor och meningsskapande processer i organisationer [The Business of Thought: Cognitive Maps and Sense-Making Processes in Organisations]*. Stockholm: Nerenius & Santérus.

Hellgren, B., & Löwstedt, J. (1998). Agency and organization: a social theory approach to cognition. In C. Eden & J.-C. Spender (eds.), *Managerial and Organizational Cognition: Theory, Methods and Research*, 40–57. Thousand Oaks, CA: Sage.

Hellgren, B., & Melin, L. (1993). The role of strategists' ways-of-thinking in strategic change processes. In J. Hendry, G. Johnson with J. Newton (eds.), *Strategic Thinking: Leadership and the Management of Change*, 47–68. Chichester: John Wiley & Sons.

Högskoleverket [Swedish Higher Education Agency]. (2006). Rapport [Report] 2006:3 R. *Högre utbildning och forskning 1945–2005. En översikt [Higher Education and Research 1945–2005: An Overview]*. Stockholm: Högskoleverket.

Holmqvist, M. (2018). *Handels. Maktelitens skola [The Stockholm School of Economics: The School of the Power Elite]*. Stockholm: Atlantis.

Hope, J., & Fraser, R. (2003). New ways of setting rewards: the beyond budgeting model. *California Management Review*, 45(4), 104–19.

Jacob, M., Hellström, T., Adler, N., & Norrgren, F. (2000). From sponsorship to partnership in academy-industry relations. *R&D Management*, 30(3), 255–62.

Jensen, M. C., & Meckling, W. H. (1976). Theory of the firm: managerial behavior, agency costs and ownership structure. *Journal of Financial Economics*, 3(4), 305–60.

Johanson, J., & Vahlne, J. E. (1977). The internationalization process of the firm: a model of knowledge development and increasing foreign market commitments. *Journal of International Business Studies, 8*(1), 23–32.

Johanson, J., & Vahlne, J. E. (1990). The mechanism of internationalisation. *International Marketing Review, 7*(4), 11–24.

Johanson, J., & Vahlne, J. E. (2009). The Uppsala internationalization process model revisited: from liability of foreignness to liability of outsidership. *Journal of International Business Studies, 40*(9), 1411–31.

Johnson, G., Langley, A., Melin, L., & Whittington, R. (2007). *Strategy as Practice: Research Directions and Resources*. Cambridge: Cambridge University Press.

Johnson, G., Melin, L., & Whittington, R. (2003). Micro strategy and strategizing: towards an activity-based view. *Journal of Management Studies, 40*(1), 3–22.

Kalling, T. (1999). *Gaining competitive advantage through information technology: a resource-based approach to the creation and employment of strategic IT resources*. PhD thesis. Lund University.

Khurana, R. (2007). *From Higher Aims to Hired Hands: The Social Transition of American Business Schools and the Unfulfilled Promise of Management as a Profession*. Princeton, NJ: Princeton University Press.

Kieser, A., & Leiner, L. (2009). Why the rigour–relevance gap in management research is unbridgeable. *Journal of Management Studies, 46*(3), 516–33.

Kogut, B., & Zander, U. (1992). Knowledge of the firm, combinative capabilities, and the replication of technology. *Organization Science, 3*(3), 383–97.

Lakemond, N., Bengtsson, L., Keld Laursen, K., & Tell, F. (2016). Match and manage: the use of knowledge matching and project management to integrate knowledge in collaborative inbound open innovation. *Industrial and Corporate Change, 25*(2), 333–52.

Larsson, R. (1993). Case survey methodology: quantitative analysis of patterns across case studies. *Academy of Management Journal, 36*(6), 1515–46.

Larsson, R., Bengtsson, L., Henriksson, K., & Sparks, J. (1998). The interorganizational learning dilemma: collective knowledge development in strategic alliances. *Organization Science, 9*(3), 285–305.

Larsson, R., & Finkelstein, S. (1999). Integrating strategic, organizational, and human resource perspectives on mergers and acquisitions: a case survey of synergy realization. *Organization Science, 10*(1), 1–26.

Latham, G. P. (2019). Perspectives of a practitioner-scientist on organizational psychology/organizational behavior. *Annual Review of Organizational Psychology and Organizational Behavior, 6*(1), 1–16.

Latour, B. (1987). *Science in Action: How to Follow Scientists and Engineers Through Society*. Boston, MA: Harvard University Press.

Lave, J., & Wenger, E. (1991). *Situated Learning: Legitimate Peripheral Participation*. Cambridge: Cambridge University Press.

Lawler III, E. E., & Benson, G. S. (2022). The practitioner-academic gap: a view from the middle. *Human Resource Management Review, 32*(1), 1–13.

Lawrence, P. R., & Lorsch, J. W. (1967). Differentiation and integration in complex organizations. *Administrative Science Quarterly, 12*(1), 1–47.

Lind, J.-I. (1993). *Kommuner som marknadsskapare. Systemskifte i praktik och teori [Municipalities as Market Makers: System Change in Practice and Theory]*. Stockholm: Kommunförbundet FoU-råd [Association of Municipalities R&D Council].

Lind, J.-I., & Rhenman, E. (1989). The SIAR school of strategic management. *Scandinavian Journal of Management, 5*(3), 167–76.

Locke, R. R. (1985). Business education in Germany: past systems and current practice. *Business History Review, 59*(2), 232–53.

Magnusson, L. (1987). Mercantilism and 'reform' mercantilism: the rise of economic discourse in Sweden during the eighteenth century. *History of Political Economy, 19*(3), 415–33.

Magnusson, L. (1992). Economics and the public interest: the emergence of economics as an academic subject during the 18th century. *Scandinavian Journal of Economics, 94*(1), S249–57.

March, J. G., & Simon, H. A. (1958). *Organizations*. New York: John Wiley & Sons.

McLaren, P. G. (2019). Stop blaming Gordon and Howell: unpacking the complex history behind the research-based model of education. *Academy of Management Learning & Education, 18*(1), 43–58.

Melin, L. (1977). *Strategisk inköpsverksamhet – organisation och interaktion [Strategic purchasing operations – organisation and interaction]*. PhD thesis. Linköping University.

Melin, L. (1985). Strategies in managing turnaround. *Long Range Planning, 18* (1), 80–6.

Melin, L. (1987). The field-of-force metaphor: a study in industrial change. *International Studies of Management & Organization, 17*(1), 24–33.

Melin, L. (1989). The field-of-force metaphor. *Advances in International Marketing, 3*(1), 161–79.

Melin, L. (1992). Internationalization as a strategy process. *Strategic Management Journal, 13*(S2), 99–118.

Miller, D., & Mintzberg, H. (1974). *Strategy formulation in context: some tentative models*. Working paper. McGill University.

Mintzberg, H. (1973). *The Nature of Managerial Work*. New York: Harper & Row.

Mintzberg, H. (1977). Strategy formulation as a historical process. *International Studies of Management & Organization, 7*(2), 28–40.

Mintzberg, H. (1978). Patterns in strategy formation. *Management Science, 24* (9), 934–48.

Mintzberg, H. (1987). The strategy concept I: five Ps for strategy. *California Management Review, 30*(1), 11–24.

Monsen, N. (2002). The case for cameral accounting. *Financial Accountability & Management, 18*(1), 39–72.

Muhic, M., & Bengtsson, L. (2021). Dynamic capabilities triggered by cloud sourcing: a stage-based model of business model innovation. *Review of Managerial Science, 15*(1), 33–54.

Nonaka, I. (1994). A dynamic theory of organizational knowledge creation. *Organization Science, 5*(1), 14–37.

Normann, R. (1969). *Variation och omorientering. En studie av innovationsförmåga [Variation and Reorientation: A Study of Innovativeness].* Stockholm: SIAR.

Normann, R. (1971). Organisational innovativeness: product variation and reorientation. *Administrative Science Quarterly, 16*(2), 203–15.

Normann, R. (1975). *Skapande företagsledning [Creative Corporate Management].* Stockholm: Aldus.

Normann, R. (1976). *Management and Statesmanship.* Stockholm: SIAR.

Normann, R. (1984). *Service Management: Stategy and Leadership in Service Business.* New York: John Wiley & Sons.

Normann, R. (1989). *Invadörernas dans – eller den oväntade konkurrensen [The Dance of the Invaders – or the Unexpected Competition].* Malmö: Liber.

Normann, R. (2001). *Reframing Business: When the Map Changes the Landscape.* Chichester: John Wiley & Sons.

Normann, R., & Ramirez, R. (1993). From value chain to value constellation: designing interactive strategy. *Harvard Business Review, 71*(4), 65–77.

Pehrsson, A. (2004). Strategy competence: a successful approach to international market entry. *Management Decision, 42*(6), 758–68.

Pehrsson, A. (2006). Business relatedness and performance: a study of managerial perceptions. *Strategic Management Journal, 27*(3), 265–82.

Pehrsson, A. (2008). Strategy antecedents of modes of entry into foreign markets. *Journal of Business Research, 61*(2), 132–40.

Pehrsson, A. (2009). Barriers to entry and market strategy: a literature review and a proposed model. *European Business Review, 21*(1), 64–77.

Pehrsson, A. (2016). Firm's strategic orientation, market context, and performance: literature review and opportunities for international strategy research. *European Business Review, 28*(4), 378–404.

Penrose, E. (1959). *The Theory of the Growth of the Firm.* Oxford: Oxford University Press.

Pierson, F. C. (1959). *The Education of American Businessmen: Ford Foundation Report.* New York: McGraw-Hill.

Porter, M. (1980). *Competitive Strategy.* New York: Free Press.

Porter, M. (1985). *Competitive Advantage.* New York: Free Press.

Porter, M. (1990). *The Competitive Advantage of Nations.* New York: Free Press.

Porter, M. E., & Sölvell, Ö. (1998). The role of geography in the process of innovation and the sustainable competitive advantage of firms. In A. D. Chandler, P. Hagström & Ö. Sölvell (eds.), *The Dynamic Firm: The Role of Technology, Strategy, Organisations and Regions*, 440–57. Oxford: Oxford University Press.

Prahalad, C. K., & Hamel, G. (1990). The core competence of the corporation. *Harvard Business Review, 68*(3), 79–91.

Prencipe, A., & Tell, F. (2001). Inter-project learning: processes and outcomes of knowledge codification in project-based firms. *Research Policy, 30*(9), 1373–94.

Pufendorf, S. von. ([1688]/1934). *De Jure Naturae et Gentium libri octo [Eight Books on the Law of Nature and Nations].* Oxford: Clarendon Press.

Quinn, J. B. (1978). Strategic change: 'logical incrementalism'. *Sloan Management Review, 20*(1), 7–21.

Regnér, P. (2003). Strategy creation in the periphery: inductive versus deductive strategy making. *Journal of Management Studies, 40*(1), 57–82.

Rehnberg, J. (2009). *The First 100 Years: Stockholm School of Economics.* Stockholm: Informationsförlaget.

Rhenman, E. (1961). *Tre uppsatser om organisation [Three essays on organisation].* Licentiate thesis. Stockholm School of Economics.

Rhenman, E. (1962). Det administrerande systemet. En organisationsmodell [The organisation as a control system]. *Ekonomisk Tidskrift [Economic Journal], 64*(3), 87–107.

Rhenman, E. (1964). *Företagsdemokrati och företagsorganisation [Corporate Democracy and Corporate Organisation].* Stockholm: Norstedts.

Rhenman, E. (1968). *Organisationsplanering. En studie av organisationskonsulter [Organisational Planning: A Study of Organisational Consultants].* Stockholm: SIAR.

Rhenman, E. (1969a). *Företaget och dess omvärld. Organisationsteori för långsiktsplanering [The Corporation and Its Environment: Organisation Theory for Long-Term Planning].* Stockholm: Bonniers.

Rhenman, R. (1969b). *Centrallasarettet. Systemanalys av ett svenskt sjukhus [The Central Hospital: System Analysis of a Swedish Hospital].* Stockholm: SIAR.

Rhenman, E., & Stymne, B. (1965). *Företagsledning i en föränderlig värld [Business Management in a Changing World]*. Stockholm: Aldus/Bonniers.

Rogers, E. M. (1983). *Diffusion of Innovations*, 3rd ed. New York: Free Press.

Rousseau, D. M. (2006). Is there such a thing as 'evidence-based management'? *Academy of Management Review, 31*(2), 256–69.

Rousseau, D. M. (2007). A sticky, leveraging, and scalable strategy for high-quality connections between organizational practice and science. *Academy of Management Journal, 50*(5), 1037–42.

Rumelt, R. P. (1974). *Strategy, Structure, and Economic Performance*. Boston, MA: Harvard Business School Press.

Rumelt, R. P, Schendel, D. E., & Teece, D. J. (1994). *Fundamental Issues in Strategy: A Research Agenda*. Boston, MA: Harvard Business School Press.

Schriber, S. (2016). Nordic strategy research: topics, theories and trends. *Scandinavian Journal of Management, 32*(4), 220–30.

Schwenk, C. R. (1982). Why sacrifice rigour for relevance? A proposal for combining laboratory and field research in strategic management. *Strategic Management Journal, 3*(3), 213–25.

Scott, W. R. (1995). *Institutions and Organizations*. Thousand Oaks, CA: Sage.

Selznick, P. (1957). *Leadership in Administration*. New York: Harper & Row.

Shani, A. B., Mohrman, S. A., Pasmore, W. A., Stymne, B., & Adler, N. (eds.) (2007). *Handbook of Collaborative Management Research*. Thousand Oaks, CA: Sage.

Simon, H. (1947). *Administrative Behavior: A Study of Decision-Making Processes in Administrative Organization*. New York: Macmillan.

Sjöstrand, S. E. (1997). *The Two Faces of Management: The Janus Factor*. Boston, MA: Cengage Learning Business Press.

Sölvell, Ö. (1987). Entry barriers and foreign penetration: emerging pattern of international competition in two electrical industries. Unpublished doctoral dissertation. Stockholm School of Economics.

Sölvell, Ö., Zander, I., & Porter, M. E. (1991). *Advantage Sweden*. Stockholm: Norstedts Juridik.

Spender, J.-C. (1996). Making knowledge the basis of a dynamic theory of the firm. *Strategic Management Journal, 17*(Winter Special Issue), 45–62.

Starkey, K., & Madan, P. (2001). Bridging the relevance gap: aligning stake-holders in the future of management research. *British Journal of management, 12*(1), S3–26.

Styhre, A., & Sundgren, M. (2005). Action research as experimentation. *Systemic Practice and Action Research, 18*(1), 53–65.

Stymne, B. (1970). *Values and Processes: A Systems Study of Effectiveness in Three Organisations*. Stockholm: SIAR.

Stymne, B. (1995). *Eric Rhenman – nydanare inom svensk företagsekonomi [Eric Rhenman – Innovator in Swedish Business Administration]*. Stockholm: SNS Förlag.

Sund, L. G., Melin, L., & Haag, K. (2015). Intergenerational ownership succession: shifting the focus from outcome measurements to preparatory requirements. *Journal of Family Business Strategy, 6*(3), 166–77.

Svalander, P.-A. (1979). *Att förnya sjukvårdens organisation [Renewing the Organisation of Health Care]*. Malmö: Liber.

Svalander, P.-A. (1982). *Primärvårdspolitiken and makten [Primary Health Care Policy and Power]*. Stockholm: Socialdepartementet.

Teece, D. J. (1986). Profiting from technological innovation: implications for integration, collaboration, licensing and public policy. *Research Policy, 15*(6), 285–305.

Teece, D. J., & Pisano, G. (1994). The dynamic capability of firms: an introduction. *Industrial and Corporate Change, 3*(3), 537–56.

Tell, F. (2000). *Organizational capabilities: a study of electrical power transmission equipment manufacturers, 1878–1990*. Doctoral dissertation. Linköping University.

Tell, F. (2011). Knowledge integration and innovation: a survey of the field. In C. Berggren, A. Bergek, L. Bengtsson, M. Hobday & J. Söderlund (eds.), *Knowledge Integration and Innovation: Critical Challenges Facing International Technology-Based Firms*, 20–59. Oxford: Oxford University Press.

Tell, F., Berggren, C., Brusoni, S., & Van de Ven, A. (2017). *Managing Knowledge Integration Across Boundaries*. Oxford: Oxford University Press.

Tengblad, S. (2003). Classic, but not seminal: revisiting the pioneering study of managerial work. *Scandinavian Journal of Management, 19*(1), 85–101.

Thompson, J. D. (1956). On building an administrative science. *Administrative Science Quarterly, 1*(1), 102–11.

Thompson, J. D. (1967). *Organizations in Action*. New York: McGraw-Hill.

Tongur, S., & Engwall, M. (2014). The business model dilemma of technology shifts. *Technovation, 34*(9), 525–35.

Vahlne, J. E. (2020). Development of the Uppsala model of internationalization process: from internationalization to evolution. *Global Strategy Journal, 10*(2), 239–50.

Vahlne, J. E., & Johanson, J. (2017). From internationalization to evolution: the Uppsala model at 40 years. *Journal of International Business Studies, 48*(9), 1087–1102.

Vahlne, J. E., & Wiedersheim-Paul, F. (1973). Economic distance: model and empirical investigation. In E. Hörnell, J.-E. Vahlne & F. Weidersheim-Paul (eds.), *Export och Utlandsetableringar [Export and Foreign Establishments]*, 81–159. Uppsala: Almqvist & Wiksell.

Van de Ven, A. H. (2002). 2001 presidential address – Strategic directions for the Academy of Management: this academy is for you! *Academy of Management Review, 27*(2), 171–84.

Van de Ven, A. H., & Johnson, P. E. (2006). Knowledge for theory and practice. *Academy of Management Review, 31*(4), 802–21.

Veblen, T. (1918). *The Higher Learning in America: A Memorandum on the Conduct of Universities by Businessmen*. New York: B. W. Huebsch.

Wadin, J. L., Ahlgren, K., & Bengtsson, L. (2017). Joint business model innovation for sustainable transformation of industries: a large multinational utility in alliance with a small solar energy company. *Journal of Cleaner Production, 160*, 139–50.

Wadström, P. (2020). *Corporate strategizing: building the group without busting the businesses*. PhD thesis. Royal Institute of Technology, Stockholm.

Wadström. P. (2022). *Advancing Strategy Through Behavioural Psychology: Creating Competitive Advantage in Relentlessly Changing Markets*. London: Kogan Page.

Wakefield, A. (2005). Books, bureaus, and the historiography of cameralism. *European Journal of Law and Economics, 19*(3), 311–20.

Welch, C., Nummela, N., & Liesch, P. (2016). Editorial – the internationalization process model revisited: an agenda for future research. *Management International Review, 56*(6), 783–804.

Whitley, R. (1984). The fragmented state of management studies: reasons and consequences. *Journal of Management Studies, 21*(3), 331–48.

Whittington, R. (1996). Strategy as practice. *Long Range Planning, 29*(5), 731–5.

Whittington, R. (2006). Completing the practice turn in strategy research. *Organization Studies, 27*(5), 613–34.

Whittington, R. (2007). Strategy practice and strategy process: family differences and the sociological eye. *Organization Studies, 28*(10), 1575–86.

Wikström, S., & Normann, R. (1994). *Knowledge and Value: A New Perspective on Corporate Transformation*. London: Routledge.

Williamson, O. E. (1985). *The Economic Institutions of Capitalism*. New York: Free Press.

Winter, S. G. (1987). Knowledge and competence as strategic assets. In D. J. Teece (ed.), *The Competitive Challenge*, 159–84. Cambridge, MA: Ballinger.

Woodward, J. (1965). *Industrial Organization: Theory and Practice*. New York: Oxford University Press.

Yin, R. K. (1984). *Case Study Research: Design and Methods*, 2nd ed. Thousand Oaks, CA: Sage.

Zander, U. (1991). *Exploiting a technological edge: voluntary and involuntary dissemination of technology.* Doctoral dissertation. Institute of International Business, Stockholm.

Cambridge Elements $\equiv$

Business Strategy

J.-C. Spender
Kozminski University

J.-C. Spender is a research Professor, Kozminski University. He has been active in the business strategy field since 1971 and is the author or co-author of 7 books and numerous papers. His principal academic interest is in knowledge-based theories of the private sector firm, and managing them.

About the Series
Business strategy's reach is vast, and important too since wherever there is business activity there is strategizing. As a field, strategy has a long history from medieval and colonial times to today's developed and developing economies. This series offers a place for interesting and illuminating research including industry and corporate studies, strategizing in service industries, the arts, the public sector, and the new forms of Internet-based commerce. It also covers today's expanding gamut of analytic techniques.

Cambridge Elements ≡

Business Strategy

Elements in the Series

Printed in the United States
by Baker & Taylor Publisher Services